BAPTISTWAY ADULT BIBLE STUDY GUIDE®

The Letters of James and John

REAL FAITH

RANDEL EVERETT
RONNIE AND RENATE HOOD
TOM HOWE
PERRY LASSITER
LEIGH ANN POWERS
BILL TINSLEY

BAPTISTWAYPRESS®

Dallas, Texas

The Letters of James and John: Real Faith—BaptistWay Adult Bible Study Guide®

BAPTISTWAY PRESS® Management Team
Executive Director, Baptist General Convention of Texas: Randel Everett
Director, Education/Discipleship Center: Chris Liebrum
Director, Bible Study/Discipleship Team: Phil Miller
Publisher, BAPTISTWAY PRESS®: Ross West

Cover and Interior Design and Production: Desktop Miracles, Inc.
Printing: Data Reproductions Corporation

First edition: September 2010
ISBN–13: 978–1–934731–55–0

How to Make the Best Use of This Issue

Whether you're the teacher or a student—

1. Start early in the week before your class meets.

2. Overview the study. Review the table of contents and read the study introduction. Try to see how each lesson relates to the overall study.

3. Use your Bible to read and consider prayerfully the Scripture passages for the lesson. (You'll see that each writer has chosen a favorite translation for the lessons in this issue. You're free to use the Bible translation you prefer and compare it with the translation chosen for that unit, of course.)

4. After reading all the Scripture passages in your Bible, then read the writer's comments. The comments are intended to be an aid to your study of the Bible.

5. Read the small articles—"sidebars"—in each lesson. They are intended to provide additional, enrichment information and inspiration and to encourage thought and application.

6. Try to answer for yourself the questions included in each lesson. They're intended to encourage further thought and application, and they can also be used in the class session itself.

If you're the teacher—

A. Do all of the things just mentioned, of course. As you begin the study with your class, be sure to find a way to help your class know the date on which each lesson will be studied. You might do this in one or more of the following ways:

- In the first session of the study, briefly overview the study by identifying with your class the date on which each lesson will be studied. Lead your class to write the date in the table of contents on page 7 and on the first page of each lesson.

- Make and post a chart that indicates the date on which each lesson will be studied.
- If all of your class has e-mail, send them an e-mail with the dates the lessons will be studied.
- Provide a bookmark with the lesson dates. You may want to include information about your church and then use the bookmark as an outreach tool, too. A model for a bookmark can be downloaded from www.baptistwaypress.org on the Resources for Adults page.
- Develop a sticker with the lesson dates, and place it on the table of contents or on the back cover.

B. Get a copy of the *Teaching Guide*, a companion piece to this *Study Guide*. The *Teaching Guide* contains additional Bible comments plus two teaching plans. The teaching plans in the *Teaching Guide* are intended to provide practical, easy-to-use teaching suggestions that will work in your class.

C. After you've studied the Bible passage, the lesson comments, and other material, use the teaching suggestions in the *Teaching Guide* to help you develop your plan for leading your class in studying each lesson.

D. You may want to get the additional adult Bible study comments—*Adult Online Bible Commentary*—by Dr. Jim Denison (president, The Center for Informed Faith, and theologian-in-residence, Baptist General Convention of Texas) that are available at www.baptistwaypress.org and can be downloaded free. An additional teaching plan plus teaching resource items are also available free at www.baptistwaypress.org.

E. You also may want to get the enrichment teaching help that is provided on the internet by the *Baptist Standard* at www.baptiststandard.com. (Other class participants may find this information helpful, too.) Call 214–630–4571 to begin your subscription to the printed or electronic edition of the *Baptist Standard*.

F. Enjoy leading your class in discovering the meaning of the Scripture passages and in applying these passages to their lives.

Writers of This Study Guide

Randel Everett is executive director, Baptist General Convention of Texas. Dr. Everett wrote lessons one and two on the Book of James. He formerly served churches in Texas, Arkansas, and Virginia and also served as founding president of the John Leland Center for Theological Studies, Arlington, Virginia. He earned master's and doctoral degrees from Southwestern Baptist Theological Seminary.

Ronnie and Renate Hood wrote lessons three and four on the Book of James. Dr. Ronnie W. Hood II is senior pastor of Canyon Creek Baptist Church, Temple, Texas. He is a graduate of Samford University, Birmingham, Alabama. Dr. Renate Viveen Hood is associate professor of Christian Studies at the University of Mary Hardin-Baylor, Belton, Texas. She earned medical science degrees in the Netherlands. The Hoods studied at New Orleans Baptist Theological Seminary, where Ronnie earned M.Div., Th.M., and Ph.D. (Church History) degrees, and Renate earned M.Div. and Ph.D. (Biblical Studies and Greek) degrees.

Tom Howe, who wrote lessons five and six on the Book of James, is the senior pastor of Birdville Baptist Church, Haltom City, Texas. Dr. Howe is a graduate of East Texas Baptist University (B.S.), Beeson Divinity School at Samford University (M. Div.) and Southwestern Baptist Theological Seminary (D. Min.).

Perry Lassiter wrote lessons seven and eight on 1 John. A graduate of Baylor University and of Southern Baptist Theological Seminary, he is a veteran curriculum writer. He served as a pastor for more than forty-five years and continues to preach and to serve churches as an interim pastor. He is a member of First Baptist Church, Ruston, Louisiana.

Leigh Ann Powers wrote lessons nine, ten, and eleven on 1 John. She is a member of First Baptist Church, Winters, Texas, where her husband serves as pastor. Leigh Ann is a graduate of Baylor University (B.S.Ed) and of Southwestern Baptist Theological Seminary (M.Div). She and her husband, Heath, have two children.

William (Bill) Tinsley wrote lesson twelve on 1 John and lesson thirteen on 2 and 3 John. He is retired as the leader of WorldconneX, the missions network created by the Baptist General Convention of Texas. Prior to this, he served as associate executive director of the Baptist General Convention of Texas; executive director of the Minnesota-Wisconsin Baptist Convention; director of missions in Denton Association, Texas; and pastor for sixteen years.

The Letters of James and John: Real Faith

Introducing

THE LETTERS OF JAMES AND JOHN:
Real Faith

General Epistles

The Letters of James and John are included in what often are referred to as the *General Epistles* of the New Testament. The *General Epistles* are thought to have been written specifically either for more than one congregation or for a congregation or congregations whose location is now unknown. A definite exception to this description is 3 John, which was written to an individual. The name *General Epistles*, though, has stuck, and it helps to distinguish these writings from Paul's letters. Included in the *General Epistles*, in addition to James and 1, 2, and 3 John, are 1 and 2 Peter and Jude.

Why Study the Letters of James and John
(or Why Study Only These Among the General Epistles?)

The main reasons for focusing on the Letters of James and John for this study are (1) length and (2) subject matter. First, limiting the study to these letters offers the opportunity to provide a fairly thorough treatment of each of them during thirteen study sessions. Second, as we will see in the study, the Book of James and the Letters of John, especially 1 John, deal with a similar major concern: *What is real faith?* Or, to state it another way, *What is real Christianity?* James and 1 John approach that concern in a rather different manner, but each provides pointed instruction on this concern that we would do well to heed.

Acts 11:26 states that "it was in Antioch that the disciples were first called 'Christians.'"[1] The assumption is that they were called "Christians" because they were like Christ. The Greek word translated "Christians" means something like *little Christs.* Are we really enough like Christ that the intent of the name "Christians" applies to us? Is our Christianity really real? If we who call ourselves "Christians" today did not already have that name, would anyone use that name to describe us? The Scriptures for this study call us to consider what real faith, real Christianity, is. More specifically, they call us to consider what real Christians are like. Further, as we sometimes say today, they call us to ask, *Do we fit the profile?*

NOTES

1. Unless otherwise indicated, all Scripture quotations in "Introducing the Letters of James and John: Real Faith" are from the New Revised Standard Version Bible.

The Book of James: Real Faith in Action

What Real Faith Looks Like

The Book of James deals with making quite plain what real faith looks like in action. As we study the Book of James, we will see quickly that we cannot accuse James of being vague. Like the Old Testament prophets, the Book of James forthrightly, specifically, practically defines how real faith acts.

The Book's Structure

The Book of James often seems to move from topic to topic rather than to develop an extended treatment of a theme. This lack of topical organization seems especially evident in James 1, with its short teaching units. The teaching units in James 2—5 are generally longer than those in James 1, although how they connect still may not be readily apparent. Even so, various ways of connecting the teaching units can be seen. Some teaching units are connected thematically. See, for example, how both 2:1–13 and 2:14–26 deal with related themes. Other teaching units are joined by key words. For example, note the word "lacking" in James 1:4 (NASB, NIV, NRSV) and the word "lacking" (NRSV) or "lacks" (NIV, NASB) in 1:5 in treating topics that seem unrelated.[1]

Which James?

James 1:1 identifies the writer to be "James." But which James? Because of the prominence in Acts and Paul's letters of "James the Lord's brother" (Galatians 1:19; see Acts 12:17), tradition has identified the author as this James. The James prominent in the Gospels, "James, the brother of John" (Acts 12:2), had been put to death by King Herod.

The Book's First Readers

James 1:1 addresses the book "To the twelve tribes in the Dispersion." This address is the most definite description we have for a specific audience for the book. The Jewish relationship is evident in the expression, and so the first intended readers may well have been Christians with a Jewish background.

 We would like to know more about where the first readers were located and what they were like. Various suggestions have been made, but the basic answer is that we do not know for sure. If we knew more, we might understand better some of the finer details of the letter. We likely will find the message of James quite clear enough, however, to cause us to ponder what we should do in response to its challenge.

THE BOOK OF JAMES: REAL FAITH IN ACTION

Lesson 1	Christian Living 101	James 1
Lesson 2	If You're Really Christian	James 2
Lesson 3	Words That Reveal Faith—or Not	James 3:1–12
Lesson 4	Want Peace? Start Here	James 3:13—4:12
Lesson 5	Living As If God Doesn't Matter	James 4:13—5:6
Lesson 6	Living Faith in Christian Community	James 5:7–20

Additional Resources for Studying the Book of James[2]

 Donald W. Burdick. "James." *The Expositors Bible Commentary.* Volume 12. Grand Rapids Michigan: Zondervan, 1981.
 Joel Gregory. *James: Faith Works.* Nashville, Tennessee: Convention Press, 1986.

Luke Timothy Johnson. "James." *The New Interpreter's Bible.* Volume XII. Nashville: Abingdon Press, 1998.

Craig S. Keener. *IVP Bible Background Commentary: New Testament.* Downers Grove, Illinois: InterVarsity Press, 1993.

Ralph P. Martin. *James.* Word Biblical Commentary. Volume 48. Dallas, Texas: Word Books, Publisher, 1988.

David Nystrom. "James." *The NIV Application Commentary.* Grand Rapids, Michigan: Zondervan, 1997.

A.T. Robertson. *Word Pictures in the New Testament.* Volume VI. Nashville, Tennessee: Broadman Press, 1933.

Harold S. Songer. "James." *The Broadman Bible Commentary.* Volume 12. Nashville, Tennessee: Broadman Press, 1972.

Foy Valentine. *Hebrews, James, 1 & 2 Peter.* Layman's Bible Book Commentary. Volume 23. Nashville, Tennessee: Broadman Press, 1981.

Curtis Vaughan. *A Study Guide: James.* Grand Rapids, Michigan: Zondervan Publishing House, 1969.

NOTES

1. Unless otherwise indicated, all Scripture quotations in "The Book of James: Real Faith in Action" are from the New Revised Standard Version Bible.

2. Listing a book does not imply full agreement by the writers or BAPTISTWAY PRESS® with all of its comments.

MAIN IDEA
Faith that is genuine calls for action in all the details of life.

QUESTION TO EXPLORE
Is our Christian faith so real that we live it out in the details of our lives?

STUDY AIM
To consider whether the Christian faith is so real to me that I live it out in the details of my life

QUICK READ
Faith that is genuine calls for action in all the details of life. Those who hear the word but whose actions are not affected have deluded themselves.

LESSON ONE
Christian Living 101

Years ago I heard a story from a Baptist pastor about a homebound member of his congregation who was found dead in her home. The pastor had gone to check on her because she had not been heard from in several days. One of the police officers who investigated her death found a stack of almost seventy-five unused prescriptions for medicines. She had gone to the doctor, who had prescribed treatment, and yet she failed to do what the doctor had said. She was merely a prescription collector.

In the first chapter of James, we are reminded that reading the Bible and failing to act on its teachings is just as foolish and deadly as collecting prescriptions without taking the medicine.[1]

JAMES 1

[1] James, a bond-servant of God and of the Lord Jesus Christ, to the twelve tribes who are dispersed abroad: Greetings. [2] Consider it all joy, my brethren, when you encounter various trials, [3] knowing that the testing of your faith produces endurance. [4] And let endurance have its perfect result, so that you may be perfect and complete, lacking in nothing. [5] But if any of you lacks wisdom, let him ask of God, who gives to all generously and without reproach, and it will be given to him. [6] But he must ask in faith without any doubting, for the one who doubts is like the surf of the sea, driven and tossed by the wind. [7] For that man ought not to expect that he will receive anything from the Lord, [8] being a double-minded man, unstable in all his ways. [9] But the brother of humble circumstances is to glory in his high position; [10] and the rich man is to glory in his humiliation, because like flowering grass he will pass away. [11] For the sun rises with a scorching wind and withers the grass; and its flower falls off and the beauty of its appearance is destroyed; so too the rich man in the midst of his pursuits will fade away. [12] Blessed is a man who perseveres under trial; for once he has been approved, he will receive the crown of life which the Lord has promised to those who love Him. [13] Let no one say when he is tempted, "I am being tempted by God"; for God cannot be tempted by evil, and He Himself does not tempt anyone. [14] But each one is tempted when he is carried away and enticed by his own lust. [15] Then when lust has conceived, it gives birth to sin;

and when sin is accomplished, it brings forth death. [16] Do not be deceived, my beloved brethren. [17] Every good thing given and every perfect gift is from above, coming down from the Father of lights, with whom there is no variation or shifting shadow. [18] In the exercise of His will He brought us forth by the word of truth, so that we would be a kind of first fruits among His creatures. [19] This you know, my beloved brethren. But everyone must be quick to hear, slow to speak and slow to anger; [20] for the anger of man does not achieve the righteousness of God. [21] Therefore, putting aside all filthiness and all that remains of wickedness, in humility receive the word implanted, which is able to save your souls. [22] But prove yourselves doers of the word, and not merely hearers who delude themselves. [23] For if anyone is a hearer of the word and not a doer, he is like a man who looks at his natural face in a mirror; [24] for once he has looked at himself and gone away, he has immediately forgotten what kind of person he was. [25] But one who looks intently at the perfect law, the law of liberty, and abides by it, not having become a forgetful hearer but an effectual doer, this man will be blessed in what he does. [26] If anyone thinks himself to be religious, and yet does not bridle his tongue but deceives his own heart, this man's religion is worthless. [27] Pure and undefiled religion in the sight of our God and Father is this: to visit orphans and widows in their distress, and to keep oneself unstained by the world.

From Skeptic to Believer (1:1)

James, a half-brother of Jesus, is traditionally thought to be the writer of this letter. James was mentioned first among the brothers of Jesus in Mark 6:3. He was not a believer until after the resurrection, when Jesus appeared to him (1 Corinthians 15:7).

Paul referred to James as the Lord's brother (Galatians 1:19) and then identified him as a leader of the church (Gal. 2:9, 12). He was the same one who presided over the Council of Jerusalem and a leader among the elders (Acts 15:13; 21:18).

God has turned many hardhearted skeptics into humble followers of Christ, including James and Paul. No one is beyond the hope of God's grace. James's humility is seen as he referred to himself, not as a brother of Jesus, but as "a bond-servant of God and of the Lord Jesus Christ."

The recipients of the letter are referred to as the twelve tribes who were scattered throughout the *Diaspora*, which would indicate they were Jewish Christians living in a Roman world. They faced the challenges of following Christ in a secular society, where they were often isolated by both their beliefs and their heritage.

Hang in There (1:2–4)

Many of James's early readers faced hardships because they were Jews living among Gentiles. They endured additional challenges from their own people when they became followers of Christ. Their faith required obedience to Jesus that appeared to be treason to Romans and blasphemy

TRIALS AND TEMPTATIONS

Believers are reminded of the inevitability of "trials" in verse 2. In verse 13, we are instructed that no one is "tempted" by God. Both of these words, *trials* and *tempted,* come from the same root word in Greek, *peirasmos.* The noun form of the word is seen in verses 2 and 12, while the verb form of the word is seen in verse 13.

The original word meant *trials,* whether good or bad. In verse 2, *trial* is obviously seen in the good sense with the intent of strengthening our faith; but in verse 13, *temptation* is the negative idea of a destructive impulse.

When confronted by a trial, we should thank God for it and be joyful, recognizing that it produces endurance. We should pray for perseverance that we may be able to hang in there until it accomplishes all God intends.

When we face temptations, we should run from them, realizing that God has already prepared a way of escape (1 Corinthians 10:13).

Persevering when faced with trials leads to steadfastness. Succumbing to temptations lead to destruction.

to Jews. Christians today who live in nations where they are in the minority often encounter the same difficulties.

In verse 2, we are told "when you encounter various trials." It doesn't say *if* but "when." Trials are inevitable. No one is immune. We face sickness, rejection, grief, hardship. Trials do not come to us as punishment but as opportunities to prove the authenticity of our faith. They can either devastate us or make us strong. James challenges us to face our trials with joy because trials produce endurance.

When challenges arise in our marriage, job, church, and school, our human nature encourages us to quit or run. Yet these situations may provide the perfect time for relationships and trust to mature and be strengthened.

Golf courses provide challenges for golfers to test their abilities—water hazards, rough, trees, sand, distance, undulating greens. For some of us, a golf ball sitting perfectly still on a tee is enough of a challenge in itself. Anyone can tell quickly whether a person is truly a golfer by watching him or her play. In life, we also face trials that test or prove us. How we respond indicates whether our faith is real or phony.

When You Don't Have a Clue (1:5–8)

Too often in life we face situations for which we are unprepared. What do we do? James tells us to seek wisdom. In James 3:13–18, we are reminded that there are two kinds of wisdom—one that is earthly, natural, and demonic; and another that is from above. Earthly wisdom is filled with jealousy and selfish ambition, but godly wisdom is peaceful, gentle, and unwavering.

Godly wisdom is accessed through prayer; "ask of God, who gives to all generously and without reproach" (James 1:5). We are to pray with confidence, knowing that God desires for us to know the truth that liberates us (John 8:31–32).

Don't Bet on Your Possessions (1:9–11)

A person who thinks security can be found in personal possessions is foolish.

Even Christians in the West appear to be running a marathon race, competing with one another and seeking to acquire more possessions than their neighbors. We are taught to believe that financial security and the accumulation of wealth will bring joy and fulfillment. Yet the race never ends. There is never enough. Fear of losing it all or being surpassed by others urges us on.

One would think that the church would not fall into this trap. However, the same favoritism of the rich is often evident even there. Most Baptists are never more than a generation or two removed from poverty, or at least humble circumstances. The poor almost always respond to the gospel first. Yet as congregations grow and members become more affluent, we quickly turn our attention away from those most receptive and favor those who are least receptive.

In James 1:9–11 and 5:1–6, we are reminded about the folly of riches. They fade away as quickly as grass withers in the sun. The person of humble means should be honored in the church, and the person with social status should be humbled. The church must resist the values of society and acknowledge that our worth is found in serving Christ.

Don't Take the Bait (1:12–18)

Satan attempts to lure us with temptations. Yet rather than bringing life, yielding to temptations brings death.

James clearly stated that God cannot be tempted by evil; neither does God tempt anyone, leading us to sin. We are tempted by our own lusts. When we give in to these evil impulses within us, they bring about destruction.

The birth of a new baby is one of the most joyful events anyone can experience. When it is learned that a child has been conceived, the family begins to anticipate and plan for the birth. The nursery is prepared. Baby clothes are purchased. Days are counted until the day of delivery. One of the greatest tragedies that can be imagined results from the death of a child at birth. Instead of joy, a family is faced with unbelievable grief.

James used this same metaphor to describe the pain of sin. When lust is conceived, it promises life and joy. There is great anticipation of fulfillment. Yet when sin is experienced, it brings heartache and death.

PRACTICAL CHRISTIANITY AS IT RELATES TO LIFE'S TRIALS

- Find strength for life's trials in the joy of the Lord
- Seek wisdom from God's word in making life decisions
- Don't fall for the world's values
- Run from temptation
- Apply the principles of God's word
- Be a lifestyle advocate for the marginalized

Christians must run from temptation. Jesus taught us to pray daily for God to not allow us to fall into temptation but for us to be delivered from evil. God is "the Father of lights" (James 1:17). Our experience with God is the opposite from temptation. He gives good and perfect gifts. When we follow God, God gives life, not death. God promises a crown of life to all who persevere.

The Prescription Won't Help Unless You Take the Medicine (1:19–27)

God's word is the law of liberty. It offers life—freedom—forgiveness. Yet it is of no value unless we act on it.

Dr. A. R. Jones, a veterinarian, was the chairman of deacons and a Sunday School teacher in the first church I served as a full-time pastor. He was one of the godliest men I have known through the years. He was a quiet man, possibly because of a lifetime struggle with stuttering. He was also a very wise man and the first person I would turn to when I needed advice.

Doc Jones was committed to the Bible and prayer. His large class of young adults was a result of his practical teaching from the Scripture. Doc would read the Bible, meditate on it, and consult commentaries. Even though he was a gifted Bible student, he was hungry to learn more. The Bible shaped his values, instructing his behavior as a man beyond reproach.

We live in a noisy world, surrounded by sounds of people, traffic, and media. We are bombarded with sexual temptations, racial prejudice, and greedy impulses from the internet, television, radio, billboards, and conversations. Bitter and jealous feelings of past hurts constantly reappear and seek to dominate our thoughts.

What will save us from these influences? We must humbly come before the word of God and seek the Lord. The Bible will instruct us, correct us, and equip us for right living (2 Timothy 3:16). Yet it is foolish to hear the word from God and then live according to the world's standards. James reminds us that this is as foolish as someone who looks at himself in the mirror and walks away without observing what he has seen. A blessed person is one who puts away all filthiness, listens to God's word, and then acts on it.

Anyone who claims to be religious and cannot even control his own speech has deluded himself. Genuine faith is expressed when we reach out to the most needy among us, like orphans and widows, and minister to them. Authentic Christ-followers, like Doc Jones, are unstained by the world but shaped by God's word.

Implications and Actions

My Louisiana grandmother made beautiful quilts. She took small pieces of cloth that appeared to me to have nothing in common and sewed them into practical works of art.

James covered many different subjects in the first chapter—trials, wisdom, humility, riches, temptation, and speech—which appear to be unrelated. Yet when one looks at the whole chapter, the pieces fit together like the symmetry of a quilt. A person of genuine faith is not just someone who talks a good game. A person of faith is one who reflects a life transformed by the grace of Christ, evidenced by a genuine concern for the needy.

QUESTIONS

1. What is the difference in trials in verse 2 and temptations in verse 13?

2. Does James's emphasis on works contradict Paul's teaching on faith alone?

3. Do you respond differently to a poor person and to a wealthy person who attends your church?

4. Are you involved in an ongoing ministry to someone in your community who has nothing to offer you in return?

NOTES ──────────────────────────────────

1. Unless otherwise indicated, all Scripture quotations in lessons 1–4 are from the New American Standard Bible (1995 edition).

FOCAL TEXT
James 2

BACKGROUND
James 2

MAIN IDEA

Rather than merely relying on what they believe about religion, Christians show their faith by acting with mercy and kindness even toward people the larger world considers insignificant.

QUESTION TO EXPLORE

What good is a faith that doesn't do any good?

STUDY AIM

To consider what my actions toward other people say about the reality of my faith

QUICK READ

Genuine faith is lived out. This truth is seen most clearly when Christians show their faith by acting with mercy and kindness even toward people the larger world considers insignificant.

LESSON TWO
If You're Really Christian

When Tillie Burgin and her family returned to the United States from South Korea after serving ten years as missionaries, they knew God had a different plan for their lives, a plan that involved Arlington, Texas. She and her friends prayed for seven years, and then on August 1, 1986, Mission Arlington began.[1]

Mission Arlington was born through the faithfulness of God's people at Tillie's home church, First Baptist Church, Arlington, Texas. That spirit of prayer still forms the foundation of everything Mission Arlington does today—more than twenty-three years later.

What is Mission Arlington doing? In 2009, 294 congregations held weekly services with an average attendance of 4,200 and 140 professions of faith. They gather people for Bible studies in apartment clubhouses, mobile homes, neighborhoods, or any place where people are open. An after-school program in twenty-six different locations served an average of 1,126 children a day.

With a multitude of social services, 6,959 volunteers from across the United States, and missionaries around the world, the Mission Arlington family lives to make a difference in the world for Christ. Physical needs of some of the neediest from the community are met through medical and dental clinics, food and furniture distribution, and a Christmas store that served 33,207 in 2009.

Mission Arlington is a modern example of the kind of real faith spoken of in James 2.

JAMES 2

[1] My brethren, do not hold your faith in our glorious Lord Jesus Christ with an attitude of personal favoritism. [2] For if a man comes into your assembly with a gold ring and dressed in fine clothes, and there also comes in a poor man in dirty clothes, [3] and you pay special attention to the one who is wearing the fine clothes, and say, "You sit here in a good place," and you say to the poor man, "You stand over there, or sit down by my footstool," [4] have you not made distinctions among yourselves, and become judges with evil motives? [5] Listen, my beloved brethren: did not God choose the poor of this world to be rich in faith and heirs of the kingdom which He promised to those who love Him? [6] But you have dishonored

the poor man. Is it not the rich who oppress you and personally drag you into court? [7] Do they not blaspheme the fair name by which you have been called? [8] If, however, you are fulfilling the royal law according to the Scripture, "You shall love your neighbor as yourself," you are doing well. [9] But if you show partiality, you are committing sin and are convicted by the law as transgressors. [10] For whoever keeps the whole law and yet stumbles in one point, he has become guilty of all. [11] For He who said, "Do not commit adultery," also said, "Do not commit murder." Now if you do not commit adultery, but do commit murder, you have become a transgressor of the law. [12] So speak and so act as those who are to be judged by the law of liberty. [13] For judgment will be merciless to one who has shown no mercy; mercy triumphs over judgment. [14] What use is it, my brethren, if someone says he has faith but he has no works? Can that faith save him? [15] If a brother or sister is without clothing and in need of daily food, [16] and one of you says to them, "Go in peace, be warmed and be filled," and yet you do not give them what is necessary for their body, what use is that? [17] Even so faith, if it has no works, is dead, being by itself. [18] But someone may well say, "You have faith and I have works; show me your faith without the works, and I will show you my faith by my works." [19] You believe that God is one. You do well; the demons also believe, and shudder. [20] But are you willing to recognize, you foolish fellow, that faith without works is useless? [21] Was not Abraham our father justified by works when he offered up Isaac his son on the altar? [22] You see that faith was working with his works, and as a result of the works, faith was perfected; [23] and the Scripture was fulfilled which says, "And Abraham believed God, and it was reckoned to him as righteousness," and he was called the friend of God. [24] You see that a man is justified by works and not by faith alone. [25] In the same way, was not Rahab the harlot also justified by works when she received the messengers and sent them out by another way? [26] For just as the body without the spirit is dead, so also faith without works is dead.

The Sin of Partiality (2:1–7)

Jesus' teachings, especially the Sermon on the Mount (Matthew 5—7), can be seen in this letter. Both Jesus and James recognized the poor as people of worth and value, even blessed (Matt. 5:3). They taught that true righteousness was greater than the righteousness of the religious leaders of their day (Matt. 5:20). Both Jesus and James referred to the demands of keeping the whole law, illustrated by the commandments concerning murder and adultery.

Practically every church claims to show no partiality. We say we welcome all who come our way. Yet most churches appear to be homogeneous; people look, dress, and speak in similar fashion. No congregation admits to favoritism, but when a person of status appears without prior notice a buzz begins throughout the church. The pastor is notified so a welcome can be expressed. However, when a homeless person shows up, ushers may try to handle the situation and send a warning to the pastor. James exposed the hypocrisy of this attitude.

James referred to the readers as brothers, speaking as a pastor rather than a harsh outsider. "Do not hold" (James 2:1) is a command in the present tense, meaning, *Don't have the habit of showing favoritism.* The word translated "favoritism" means literally *to lift up a face.* The idea is that Christians don't look at someone's face to decide whether they'll treat them well.

Two men of contrasting styles enter the "assembly" (Greek word for *synagogue*). One is extravagantly dressed with fine clothes and a gold ring. The other is shabby, with the implication he was also dirty. Special attention is given to the wealthy person; he is ushered to a seat of honor. The poor man is dismissed away from the attention of others. In the Greek text, the emphatic pronoun for "you" (*su*) is used in both situations. "'*You* sit here in a good place,' and you say to the poor man, '*You* stand over there, or sit down by my footstool. . .'" (2:3, italics added for emphasis). The verb "sit" used for the man of honor is present tense, indicating continuous action. The poor man is told to "stand" (the Greek aorist tense, indicating completed action). The man of honor is invited, *You come sit in this special seat for as long as you wish.* The poor person is pushed aside, *You stand over there.*

James reminded his beloved brothers, "Did not God choose the poor of this world to be rich in faith and heirs of the kingdom which He promised to those who love Him?" (2:5).

The poor were abundant in the New Testament church. It was unusual for a wealthy person to appear. When Jesus said that the poor in spirit are blessed (Matt. 5:3), he was not saying that poverty is a blessing. He was indicating that one who is hungry or grieving is much more likely to respond to the hope of the gospel than one whose life is full. The

FAITH AND WORKS

Is there a conflict between James and Paul on the subjects of faith and works?

Paul wrote

- "For we maintain that a man is justified by faith apart from works of the Law" (Romans 3:28).

- ". . . A man is not justified by the works of the Law but through faith in Christ Jesus, even we have believed in Christ Jesus, so that we may be justified by faith in Christ, and not by the works of the Law; since by the works of the Law no flesh will be justified" (Galatians 2:16).

Paul quoted Genesis 15:6 in Romans 4:9, "For we say, 'Faith was credited to Abraham as righteousness,'" as proof that Abraham's faith made him righteous.

In James 2:17, 20–21, James taught there is no faith without works. In verse 21, he referred to Abraham being "justified by works when he offered up Isaac his son on the altar." Then, in verse 23, James, like Paul, cited Genesis 15:6: ". . . The Scripture was fulfilled which says, 'And Abraham believed God, and it was reckoned to him as righteousness. . . .'"

Taken out of context these statements may appear contradictory. Yet they are not. Paul was speaking on the subject of justification, and James was speaking about genuine faith showing itself in good works. James was not speaking of the ceremonial law leading to salvation, but of the kind of works that are the result of genuine faith.

church grows most rapidly among people who face hardships. A Korean pastor told me near the time I was writing this lesson that the church in South Korea appears to be at a plateau after decades of incredible expansion. The church has grown through persecution and poverty, and now it faces the greatest challenge—prosperity.

Our society exalts some traits above others, including looks, wealth, status, power, athleticism, and intelligence. The ones possessing more of these qualities are entitled to different standards and given greater perks. They are often immune to the scrutiny and even demands expected of others.

James pointed out that it was ironic that the church would favor those who oppressed them and neglect the ones who were in greatest need. Even today the church sometimes honors celebrities who blaspheme the Lord with their speech and actions. Yet true faith looks beyond a person's exterior and holds kingdom values rather than falling into the dangerous trap of favoritism.

The Royal Law (2:8–13)

True people of faith are to fulfill the royal law, "You shall love your neighbor as yourself" (James 2:8). It is the *royal* law because it is the king of all laws and because it is the law of the King. Jesus summarized the Law and the Prophets with the Golden Rule (Matt. 7:12). He said all the Law and the Prophets hang on the law of love (Matt. 22:40).

A Dallas disc jockey announced he would practice the command to love others as much as he loves himself, but he said he had to quit before lunch because no one else could stand that much affection.

Paul reminded the Philippians, "Do nothing from selfishness or empty conceit, but with humility of mind regard one another as more important than yourselves; do not merely look out for your own personal interests, but also for the interests of others" (Philippians 2:3–4). Jesus gave a new commandment, "that you love one another, even as I have loved you . . . By this all men will know that you are My disciples, if you have love for one another" (John 13:34–35).

To show partiality is sin. When we violate any part of the law, we are sinners. A man cannot be 99% faithful to his wife. Either he is 100% faithful or he is unfaithful. Since we are all guilty under the law, we should live by the law of liberty. Only mercy triumphs over judgment.

Faith and Works (2:14–26)

I still have a Chuck Colson quote from an article in *Christianity Today* more than thirty years ago (7/21/78). It is truer today than when it was written. "Religion is increasing its influence on society but morality is losing its influence. The secular world would seem to offer abundant evidence that religion is not greatly affecting our lives." Colson referred to an interview of Billy Graham by a Dutch telecaster. The telecaster said, "We read all about people in America being born again. . . . Yet we also see in America abortion on the increase, deterioration of the family structure, the crime rate increases. How is it that so many can be born again and your society still be so sick?"

Many people from around the world equate the United States with Christianity. When they observe our violence, extravagance, greed, and immorality they cannot separate it from the faith we claim. This contrast creates a stumbling block that keeps people from turning to Christ. Yet James clearly teaches that a faith without works is dead. Genuine faith is transformational. When Christ is in us, we begin to take on the values and characteristics of Christ.

PUTTING FAITH INTO ACTION

- Recognize that God loves you and can be trusted
- Allow Christ to shape your attitudes and behavior by spending time each day in Bible study and prayer
- When you encounter anyone who may appear to be an outcast in society, try to imagine how Christ would respond to him or her
- Serve as a greeter in your church, and make a point to be sure every person who appears at your church is welcomed with Christ's love

If you want to understand the nature of a dog, put a cat in front of it. If you want to know whether a person's faith is genuine, observe the person's reaction to another person in need. How can a person overlook a child who is hungry and pretend to be interested in the child's eternity? How can we be committed to missions in a foreign land and tolerant of unjust laws and practices in our own communities?

The faith (belief) James referred to in this chapter is a false faith. Even the demons believe and shudder (James 2:19). The word "shudder" means *to bristle up*, like hair standing on its end with terror.

Abraham believed God and offered up his son Isaac on the altar (Genesis 22). Rahab was a prostitute but believed God and sheltered the Hebrew spies (Joshua 2). True faith is belief in action.

In Matthew 25:31–46, Jesus described the separation of the sheep and the goats. The criterion for dividing the righteous from the unrighteous is their compassion for the needy. Yet these works didn't earn them salvation. The righteous didn't even know they were feeding and clothing Jesus. The good works were evidence of their faith, not meritorious. Abraham didn't offer Isaac to impress God; he did it because he trusted God.

Implications and Actions

In James 2, "faith" is not used in the sense of genuine, saving faith. Rather it is demonic (James 2:19), useless (2:20), and dead (2:26). Such so-called faith is a mere intellectual acceptance of certain truths without trust in Christ as Savior. James was also not saying that a person is saved by works and not by genuine faith. Rather, he was saying, to use Martin Luther's thoughts, that a person is justified (declared righteous before God) by faith alone, but not by a faith that is alone. "Genuine faith will produce good deeds, but only faith in Christ saves."[2]

QUESTIONS

1. What examples of favoritism appear in your church?

2. What is "the royal law" (James 2:8)? How does it relate to the Ten Commandments?

3. Do Romans 1:17, "the righteous man shall live by faith," and James 2:24, "a man is justified by works and not by faith alone," contradict each other?

4. Are there folks in your church community who will not feel welcome in your worship services?

5. Who are the marginalized in your community?

6. What can you do to share the love of Christ with one of the marginalized in your community?

NOTES ──

1. See www.missionarlington.org. Accessed 4/19/10.

2. *The NIV Study Bible, New International Version* (Grand Rapids, Michigan: Zondervan Bible Publishers, 1985), 1882.

FOCAL TEXT
James 3:1–12

BACKGROUND
James 3:1–12

MAIN IDEA

Words are powerful and serve as indicators of the nature and reality of our faith.

QUESTION TO EXPLORE

What do your words reveal about the reality of your faith?

STUDY AIM

To identify what my spoken and written words suggest about my faith

QUICK READ

Believers must be careful with words, for they can both build up and tear down people. Our words never should bring disunity among believers but rather express our faith.

LESSON THREE
Words That Reveal Faith—or Not

Young Larry had a stuttering problem. The letters *L* and *P* were especially hard for him. Naturally, it did not help that his name was Larry, who attended Plymouth-Whitemarsh Junior and Senior High School in Pennsylvania.

Larry recalls the time when he was elected president of the junior high student body in ninth grade. All of the seventh, eighth, and ninth graders—several hundred students—were gathered together for the induction ceremony. Larry stood next to the principal on stage for the induction ceremony and was to repeat the words, "I, Larry Crabb of Plymouth-Whitemarsh Junior High School, do hereby promise. . . ." Larry repeated, "I, L-L-L-L-Larry Crabb of P-P-P-P-Plymouth-Whitemarsh Junior High School, do hereby p-p-p-p-promise. . . ." He was so embarrassed that he decided then and there that public speaking was not for him.

A short time later his church celebrated the Lord's Supper. His church had a custom that young men would pray over the elements. It was Larry's turn to pray. He remembers nervously thanking the Father for hanging on the cross and praising Christ for bringing the Spirit from the grave, all the while stuttering.

When the service ended Larry headed straight for the door in utter embarrassment. However, Jim Dunbar, an older, godly man arrived at the door first. Mr. Dunbar grabbed his arm. Larry anticipated a sharp reprimand. To his surprise he felt Dunbar's arm on his shoulder. Larry turned and looked into his eyes. The wise, old saint said, "Larry, there is one thing I want you to know. Whatever you do for the Lord, I'm behind you one thousand percent." Larry went on his way in great relief.[1] Today Dr. Larry Crabb is a well-known author who speaks all over the world. Jim Dunbar's words made all the difference in his life.

As James turned his attention from discussing faith and works in James 2:14–26 to discussing the purity of speech in James 3:1–12, the transition seems unclear at first sight. However, James took up a theme he discussed in an earlier part of his letter. At the beginning of the letter, in chapter 1, James spoke of the bridling of the tongue as an indicator of the worth of one's religion (James 1:26). More specifically, James encouraged the recipients of his letter to be slow to speak (1:19). When readdressing this theme of wise usage of the tongue in chapter 3, he ventured deeply into issues of the impact of the spoken word on the members of the church. Beginning with teachers in the church, James made clear the pitfalls of bad speech. The tongue, or speech, is central to the work of teachers.[2] Thus, James wrote as if holding up a mirror before teachers, and all believers.

JAMES 3:1–12

[1] Let not many of you become teachers, my brethren, knowing that as such we will incur a stricter judgment. [2] For we all stumble in many ways. If anyone does not stumble in what he says, he is a perfect man, able to bridle the whole body as well. [3] Now if we put the bits into the horses' mouths so that they will obey us, we direct their entire body as well. [4] Look at the ships also, though they are so great and are driven by strong winds, are still directed by a very small rudder wherever the inclination of the pilot desires. [5] So also the tongue is a small part of the body, and yet it boasts of great things. See how great a forest is set aflame by such a small fire! [6] And the tongue is a fire, the very world of iniquity; the tongue is set among our members as that which defiles the entire body, and sets on fire the course of our life, and is set on fire by hell. [7] For every species of beasts and birds, of reptiles and creatures of the sea, is tamed and has been tamed by the human race. [8] But no one can tame the tongue; it is a restless evil and full of deadly poison. [9] With it we bless our Lord and Father, and with it we curse men, who have been made in the likeness of God; [10] from the same mouth come both blessing and cursing. My brethren, these things ought not to be this way. [11] Does a fountain send out from the same opening both fresh and bitter water? [12] Can a fig tree, my brethren, produce olives, or a vine produce figs? Nor can salt water produce fresh.

The Danger of Teaching (3:1–2)

In reading James 3:1, one realizes immediately that James was addressing a church community. In the opening of the letter, this community was addressed as "the twelve tribes who are dispersed abroad" (1:1). In James 3:1, James addressed his readers with the plural form of "you." In the second half of the verse, he addressed them as "we," and says, "as such we will incur. . . ." He thereby counted himself among the group he was addressing. James called the people *adelphoi* or *brethren*. This title was used for fellow Christians. Thus this clearly is an address to the church at large to avoid many of them becoming teachers.

One might ask whether James was aiming this verse at those believers who at that time were not yet teachers in the church, or whether he indirectly sought to speak to those who were now teaching. Furthermore, he might also have been reprimanding those who were observing teachers in the church but could not control their tongues themselves. Either way, James laid out a sobering, shared understanding in the early church—those who teach will bring on themselves a stricter judgment. This concept of judgment is a grim reality. Yet who exactly gives this judgment? Does the judgment come at the hand of God? Or does the judgment come at the hand of other Christians on judgment day? Given the somewhat Jewish Christian setting, judgment by God appears most likely.

In a genuinely pastoral way, James counted himself among the teachers of the church when he confessed that all—himself included—"stumble" in many ways. He next proposed that if a person did not stumble in speech (teaching), that person would be perfect (as a teacher). James thus admitted that no person, including himself, was perfect. The way in which the word "stumble" is used here in the original language shows that the situation painted by James was not hypothetical but rather currently ongoing. At the time James wrote his letter, certain teachers in the church had lost control of their words even to the extent that they taught false doctrine.

The Power of the Tongue (3:3–9)

James 3:3–4 gives two illustrations of the power of the tongue in terms of its effect on a congregation. A bit in a horse's mouth directs the massive animal (3:3). In like manner the words of a teacher direct an entire body of believers. Furthermore, James instructed that a small rudder can direct an entire ship with little effort (3:4). Likewise, the words of a teacher can direct an entire church.

Compared to a bit in a horse's mouth and a rudder in a ship, a tongue is a small part of the human body. However, the illustrations in James

3:3–4 are not meant to be taken in the sense that a tongue controls a human body. Rather, the point of the illustrations is made in verse 5—the tongue, the source of speech and thus of words and teaching, is very small but powerful. James's illustrations highlight the great consequences of even the smallest bit of wrong teaching. In verse 5, James claimed that the tongue boasts of great things. Boasting of self or self-accomplishments was looked down on both in the first-century culture and in the New Testament (Romans 3:27; 1 Corinthians 3:21; Ephesians 2:9). Thus, this boasting of the tongue is unfit for a believer. The "great things" to which James referred are likely the teachings of the teachers who spoke with great exaggeration.

James next discussed the potential negative power of the tongue (James 3:5). The tongue is presented as an instrument capable of sinful expressions. James claimed that the tongue in this case is set on fire "by hell" (3:6). "Hell" refers to the Hebrew *Valley of Hinnom*, a place with a bad reputation in the Old Testament and understood as referring to a place of eternal punishment.[3]

James next stated that people are able to tame all created species, but a person cannot control the tongue. The thought that the tongue is like an uncontrollable animal was common in ancient literature.[4] The recipients

SHIPS IN THE NEW TESTAMENT WORLD

Vessels that carried only passengers did not exist in the ancient world. All ships in the New Testament world were built for cargo. All people aboard the vessel helped with everything that had to be done on the ship.

Due to weather concerns, the sailing season was limited to the period from May to October. The ships had one huge, square mainsail, a small triangular topsail, and a small foresail. The sailors handled the sails. The helmsman controlled the guiding of the ship. Rather than doing so with a rudder that connected to a wheel, guiding the ship was done by pushing or pulling on tiller bars socketed into steering oars on each quarter. The overall handling of the ship was in the hands of the sailing master.

Ships existed in various sizes. Yet even the smaller ones had a galley for cooking. Ships as large as 180 feet in length and more than 45 feet wide were known to sail the Mediterranean Sea.[5]

APPLYING JAMES'S WORDS

To apply James's words in your daily walk:

- Consider the power of your words before you let them come out of your mouth
- Ask yourself whether your words encourage or discourage
- Ask yourself whether your words reflect the attitude of Christ (Philippians 2:5–8)
- Listen to your words in an effort to determine whether you need Christ to cleanse your heart

of the letter would relate well to James's point and perhaps take control of their tongues.

James had the church in mind when he said that with the tongue "we [believers in the church] bless the Lord and Father, and with it we curse those who are made in the likeness of God" (3:9, NRSV). The words "bless" and "curse," in the grammar of the original language of the New Testament, convey a sense of being both current and ongoing actions (3:9). Thus the tongue or speech to which James referred was currently used in a double-minded fashion. As James noted, such a mixture of evil and good words created disunity in the church.

The Duality of the Mouth (3:10–12)

James next focused on the effects of evil words in order to convince the recipients of the letter to control the tongue. Perhaps the words of Jesus as recorded in Matthew come to mind here, "But the things that proceed out of the mouth come from the heart. . ." (Matt. 15:18). Thus "the mouth" that speaks both blessings and curses reveals the person to be "double-minded," as described in James 1:8. Double-mindedness does not befit a person of faith.

In verse 10, the mouth reveals its source, the heart and the contents of the heart, whether evil or good. James's following illustrations describe sources that can yield only one product. A spring produces either fresh or salt water. A fig tree can produce only figs, and a vine can produce only its specific fruit. Believers likewise are single-hearted and yield good fruit, never a mixture of good and evil.

Implications and Actions

In a way, all believers are teachers. We teach those around us, in both our actions and our words. Thus we must be aware of the power of our words. With our words we can build up people, or we can break down people. We can strengthen our witness for Christ with our words, or we can weaken our witness for the Lord with our words. We can increase the unity of the church with our speech, or we can divide the church with our speech. In what way do your words reveal the reality of the faith in your heart today?

QUESTIONS

1. Think of words spoken to you when you were young, words that shaped who you are today. Why did these words have an impact on you?

2. Is the manner in which you say something as important as what you say? Why or why not?

3. Are written words more or less powerful than spoken words?

4. Why does the nature of the tongue make teaching a serious matter, not to be done by just any person?

5. In what ways do believers' words reveal the reality of their faith?

NOTES

1. Lawrence J. Crabb, Jr. and Dan B. Allender, *Encouragement: The Key to Caring* (Grand Rapids, MI: Zondervan Publishing House, 1984), 23–25.

2. Kurt A. Richardson, *The New American Commentary: James* (Nashville, TN: Broadman & Holman Publishers, 1997), 147.

3. Douglas J. Moo, *The Tyndale New Testament Commentaries: James* (Grand Rapids, MI: Wm. B. Eerdmans Publishing Co., 1985), 126.

4. Ralph P. Martin, *Word Biblical Commentary: James* (Waco, TX: Word Books, 1988), 117.

5. Lionel Casson, *Travel in the Ancient World* (Baltimore, MD: The Johns Hopkins University Press, 1994), 149–159.

FOCAL TEXT
James 3:13—4:12

BACKGROUND
James 3:13—4:12

MAIN IDEA
Selfish and self-centered behaviors bring conflict and are not in accord with the Christian way of life.

QUESTION TO EXPLORE
What are we doing that causes conflict with our fellow human beings, even fellow Christians?

STUDY AIM
To identify selfish and self-centered behaviors of mine that are causing conflict with my fellow human beings, even fellow Christians

QUICK READ
Believers must choose godly wisdom rather than earthly wisdom. Godly wisdom begins by submitting to God and results in peace among believers.

LESSON FOUR
Want Peace? Start Here

Several years ago an average-sized Baptist church was plagued with bitterness and disputing. The previous pastor had left, and several members had fallen into the rut of focusing on their wishes for the church at the expense of unity. The church was blessed with the coming of a seasoned pastor who had years of pastoral chaplaincy experience. This pastor—humble, wise, and a good observer—took time to familiarize himself with his new flock. After praying and seeking godly wisdom, he focused on a main area of disunity—the monthly business meeting.

The wise pastor had a clever idea. He decided the church would celebrate the Lord's Supper following each business meeting. After just a few times, the tone of the meetings began to change. People began to realize that their disputing would be followed by focus on the sacrificial death of Christ as they would commemorate Christ's death on the cross and his resultant forgiveness for those who accepted his offer. Finally, a radical truth dawned on those believers with bitterness: How could they continue to focus on self if the Lord himself had given his all? How could believers break bread together and yet harbor bitterness in their hearts? How could they any longer level angry words at one another during the business meeting and next celebrate the love of Christ who poured out his life's blood? In time, hearts were healed, relationships were mended, and peace returned among the members of the congregation.

At the beginning of chapter 3, James discussed the power of words and the condition of the heart. In the second half of chapter 3, James shifted the focus to earthly and heavenly wisdom and decision making. These sources of one's wisdom are recognized by fruit in the believer's life. James concluded that when God is the source of wisdom and sources of conflict are recognized, one can live a godly lifestyle that leads to peace.

JAMES 3:13–18

[13] Who among you is wise and understanding? Let him show by his good behavior his deeds in the gentleness of wisdom. [14] But if you have bitter jealousy and selfish ambition in your heart, do not be arrogant and so lie against the truth. [15] This wisdom is not that which comes down from above, but is earthly, natural, demonic. [16] For where jealousy and selfish ambition exist, there is disorder

and every evil thing. [17] But the wisdom from above is first pure, then peaceable, gentle, reasonable, full of mercy and good fruits, unwavering, without hypocrisy. [18] And the seed whose fruit is righteousness is sown in peace by those who make peace.

JAMES 4:1–12

[1] What is the source of quarrels and conflicts among you? Is not the source your pleasures that wage war in your members? [2] You lust and do not have; so you commit murder. You are envious and cannot obtain; so you fight and quarrel. You do not have because you do not ask. [3] You ask and do not receive, because you ask with wrong motives, so that you may spend it on your pleasures. [4] You adulteresses, do you not know that friendship with the world is hostility toward God? Therefore whoever wishes to be a friend of the world makes himself an enemy of God. [5] Or do you think that the Scripture speaks to no purpose: "He jealously desires the Spirit which He has made to dwell in us"? [6] But He gives a greater grace. Therefore it says, "God is opposed to the proud, but gives grace to the humble." [7] Submit therefore to God. Resist the devil and he will flee from you. [8] Draw near to God and He will draw near to you. Cleanse your hands, you sinners; and purify your hearts, you double-minded. [9] Be miserable and mourn and weep; let your laughter be turned into mourning and your joy to gloom. [10] Humble yourselves in the presence of the Lord, and He will exalt you. [11] Do not speak against one another, brethren. He who speaks against a brother or judges his brother, speaks against the law and judges the law; but if you judge the law, you are not a doer of the law but a judge of it. [12] There is only one Lawgiver and Judge, the One who is able to save and to destroy; but who are you who judge your neighbor?

The Source of Wisdom (3:13–18)

James asked, "Who among you is wise and understanding?" (James 3:13). Before seeking an answer to the question, one must determine to whom the question was addressed. Two main possibilities are likely. James could be referring to the church in general, or he could be referring to the teachers within the church (3:1).

Verse 14 begins with the word "but" in order to contrast bitter wisdom with gentle wisdom in verse 13. According to verse 15, the bitter wisdom described in verse 14 is "earthly," whereas the gentle wisdom described in verse 13b is "from above." Wisdom "from above," heavenly wisdom, is goodness revealing "gentleness" (3:13). Earthly wisdom is jealous and selfish (3:14).

Verses 14 and 16 are closely connected. The "jealousy and selfish ambition" characteristic of earthly wisdom mentioned in verse 14 leads to disorder and evil and multiplies wickedness within a group.

Next, James listed the fruit of heavenly wisdom (3:17–18). The list serves as a picture of the healthy church, in which all believers are living as true citizens of the kingdom of God. Those who possess heavenly wisdom also seek purity and peace. The words of Jesus' Sermon on the Mount come to mind, "Blessed are the peacemakers. . ." (Matt. 5:9).

PEACE IN THE NEW TESTAMENT

God is the giver of peace (Numbers 6:24–26). This peace, *shalom* in Hebrew, has the idea of wholeness or well-being (Num. 25:12; Jeremiah 14:13).

Isaiah described the Messiah as "Prince of Peace" (Isaiah 9:6). The birth of Christ was accompanied by a heavenly host declaring peace on earth (Luke 2:13–14). God began an earth-shaking movement toward peace at the birth of Christ. In the Beatitudes, Jesus said, "Blessed are the peacemakers. . ." (Matthew 5:9).

In the New Testament, the Greek word *eirene* is used to express a sense of peace. However, in classical Greek *eirene* meant the absence of striving. In the New Testament culture, the Romans believed in the idea of *pax Romana*, meaning *the peace of Rome*, which meant the absence of trouble or war. The New Testament, however, brings the Old Testament idea of *shalom* into the Greek sense of *eirene* in order to contrast the peace of Christ with the peace the world offers. James contrasted worldly wisdom that leads to chaos with wisdom's gentle peacemaking (James 3:13–18).

The Source of Conflicts (4:1–6)

James ended chapter 3 with an exhortation that peace is available to those who pursue peace. However, he was addressing hearers whose lust for conflict was hindering the peace of the congregation.

James discussed the sources of conflict within earthly wisdom. These sources keep believers from experiencing peace and life-giving relationships. When believers focus on selfish pleasures and desires, wars and arguments result. Consequently, the pattern of sin becomes prevalent in a church in which believers rely on earthly wisdom (note James 1:15).

In James 4:3, the words, "You ask and do not receive," refer to James 1:5–8. There James advised, "if any of you lacks wisdom, let him ask of God, who gives to all generously . . . But he must ask in faith without any doubting . . . ." The people did not receive, James said, because they asked in the wrong spirit, desiring only pleasures. Earthly wisdom began a process in the lives of believers that James sought to confront.

James called those who seek selfish pleasures rather than godly wisdom (4:4) "adulteresses" who sought friendship with the world. In James's male-dominated world, why did he address the people as "adulteresses"? The question finds its answer in the Old Testament, in which the relationship between the Israelites and the God of Israel often is portrayed with language about marriage (Isaiah 54:5; Jeremiah 3:14). Israel's unfaithfulness to her God was compared to adultery (Jer. 3:8; Ezekiel 23:35–37), making Israel an "adulteress." James thus characterized a part of his audience as unfaithful people of God. If the people were not faithful to God, then the alternative was that they were having a relationship with the world that was not acceptable for believers.

In verse 6, James cited a word of wisdom from the Old Testament Book of Proverbs. God resists the proud "but gives grace to the humble" (Proverbs 3:34). Stress is placed on humility, which enables one to turn from unfaithful ways and begin to experience the grace and forgiveness of God.

The Source of Godliness (4:7–12)

The statement in verse 7, "Submit therefore to God," refers back to verse 6. Why should one submit to God? Because, as James explained there,

God opposes the proud "BUT GIVES GRACE TO THE HUMBLE" (4:6). Thus believers must humbly surrender to God, seeking God's wisdom. In thus submitting to God, one is able to resist the devil. James was convinced that the evil one would flee when believers resisted. Continuing the thought of resisting the devil, James next instructed readers to "draw near to God." While the devil would flee, God would draw near. If believers truly focused on their Maker rather than being double-minded, their lives likewise would be influenced by one main source of wisdom—God.

In verses 11–12, James provided one additional item of practical guidance for humbling oneself before the Lord: one must recognize that

---

FRUIT IN THE BELIEVER'S LIFE

Fruit of Wisdom from Above (James 3:17)

- "Pure"
- "Peaceable"
- "Gentle"
- "Reasonable"
- "Full of mercy and good fruit"
- "Unwavering"
- "Without hypocrisy"

Fruit of the Spirit (Galatians 5:22)

- "Love"
- "Joy"
- "Peace"
- "Patience"
- "Kindness"
- "Goodness"
- "Faithfulness"
- "Gentleness"
- "Self-control"

refusing to "speak against" other believers is a prerequisite to achieving true peace. In chapter 3, James had discussed the destructive power of words. If one's words are hindering believers' peace, one must remember that God is the judge and begin a life of holy conversation.

Implications and Actions

We have learned about the nature of earthly wisdom from James and how its selfishness can wreck the local church and the lives of individual believers and those around them. We cannot sit around idle and allow the Lord's church to suffer disunity. Heavenly wisdom is gentle and calls for us to examine ourselves and stop subtle, selfish desires that hinder unity and peace. The lists in James 3:14–17 give direction in examining our lives. When we submit our sources of conflict to God and seek God's peace, we can be assured that God will draw near to us.

QUESTIONS

1. What is wisdom?

2. What are examples of self-centered behaviors among believers that divide a church?

3. What are examples of behaviors and attitudes among believers that will bring peace in a church and unite believers?

4. In what sense can wisdom lead to either peace or disunity?

5. How can believers shift their hearts toward godly wisdom and away from earthly wisdom?

MAIN IDEA

To live as if time goes on forever and to accumulate possessions as if they are what's truly important in life exemplify the foolishness of trying to live without God.

QUESTION TO EXPLORE

In what ways do people foolishly presume they are self-sufficient and live as if God doesn't matter?

STUDY AIM

To identify ways for using time and money most wisely instead of foolishly

QUICK READ

How much does being a Christian affect the way we really live and think? How much do we consider God in our actions and plans?

LESSON FIVE
Living As If God Doesn't Matter

51

Do we claim faith in God but actually live as if God doesn't matter? The passage of Scripture for this study calls us to face this question in specific ways.[1]

JAMES 4:13–17

[13] Now listen, you who say, "Today or tomorrow we will go to this or that city, spend a year there, carry on business and make money." [14] Why, you do not even know what will happen tomorrow. What is your life? You are a mist that appears for a little while and then vanishes. [15] Instead, you ought to say, "If it is the Lord's will, we will live and do this or that." [16] As it is, you boast and brag. All such boasting is evil. [17] Anyone, then, who knows the good he ought to do and doesn't do it, sins.

JAMES 5:1–6

[1] Now listen, you rich people, weep and wail because of the misery that is coming upon you. [2] Your wealth has rotted, and moths have eaten your clothes. [3] Your gold and silver are corroded. Their corrosion will testify against you and eat your flesh like fire. You have hoarded wealth in the last days. [4] Look! The wages you failed to pay the workmen who mowed your fields are crying out against you. The cries of the harvesters have reached the ears of the Lord Almighty. [5] You have lived on earth in luxury and self-indulgence. You have fattened yourselves in the day of slaughter. [6] You have condemned and murdered innocent men, who were not opposing you.

Making Plans as Though God Doesn't Matter (4:13–14)

What plans have you made lately? What job to take? What to spend your money on this month? Whom to date? Making plans in life is both reasonable and important. Even Jesus spoke parables about planning: (1) laying a proper foundation when making plans (Luke 6:47–49); and (2) considering the cost when making plans (Luke 14:28–30). Making plans is good, but Christians must always include God in their decision-making process. Sadly, Christians often make plans without considering what God thinks. We even ask God to bless the plans we made without first seeking what God wanted for us all along, thereby asking God to bless something God may not want in our lives.

James warned Christians to be careful not to make plans apart from thinking about God. Verse 13 seems like a reasonable plan to most business people today, perhaps even admirable. A person making such plans seems to be a goal-setter having great initiative; however, James was quick to be harsh about such thinking. This plan seems to be a business trip only interested in making money. Christians (even Christian business people) must consider other factors in making such plans: What is God's will for me? How will I be serving God? How will I be a blessing to others? What potential temptations or traps will affect my Christian faith?

Business people understand *return on investment* (ROI). More is at stake than the return on investment of one trip. James reminds us that our lives are uncertain and temporary. He used the imagery of life being a "mist' or a *vapor*. Billions of vapors (people) have come and gone since he wrote these words. Each person had hopes, plans, and return on that which they had invested their lives. Although the collective good is still around, little evidence remains of the individual accomplishments of virtually all of those billions of vapor. Little of what is being done on earth now will matter one day in the future. The great exception is that which is eternal. Christians have a greater return on investment. Nothing in this world compares to the reward that waits in heaven.

Making plans as though God doesn't matter is shortsighted. The best results this world can offer are temporary. Keeping God in the planning process allows Christians to reap a much greater return, an eternal one. This does not mean we do not have to make plans as Christians. Paul was a planner. He had made plans to go to Phrygia, Galatia, Asia, and Bithynia but was stopped by God from doing so (Acts 16:6–10). He allowed God to redirect his work to Macedonia. That did not stop Paul from continuing to make plans. He later wrote that he planned to go to Rome and then on to Spain (Romans 15:23–24). Paul made it to Rome, but whether he made it any further is uncertain. He made his plans based on the fact that God mattered to him.

Thinking as Though God Doesn't Matter (4:15–17)

James started verse 15 with "instead" as a way of showing that there must an alternate way of thinking contrasted to those who think as though God does not matter. He was setting up the contrast of how a Christian should view the world to how non-Christians view the world. The Christian worldview must always include God.

James began by saying that the Christian mindset is shaped by the Lord's will. *God willing* is more than a catch phrase. Christians are frauds if they make their own plans and then carelessly add the words *God willing*. First, we need to be determined to *learn* the will of God. Also, we need to have an equal determination to *do* the will of God, allowing God's will to saturate all our thinking. Christians cannot have two personas, one that includes God and one that does not; that would be a double-minded Christian. James warned against that way of thinking, calling such people "unstable" (James 1:8) and "sinners" (4:8).

The perfect example is Jesus, who knew the will of the Father was for him to go to the cross. He agreed to do it even though he did not want to

---

BUSINESS ETHICS

James's warnings are especially challenging in the current business climate. The modern economic machine has little regard for what matters to God. Corporate greed and lies get constant coverage in the media, leaving the impression that these are the only ways to do business. Inequalities of wealth and justice across the globe demonstrate that the bottom line tends to be the most important thing in business.

Christians operate in the same system as everyone else. Being a Christian and at the same time being a successful business person does not have to be a contradiction. A Christian should always maintain the ethics James described, even if he or she is the minority in a mass of unprincipled, cut-throat business combatants.

Living as though God matters carries over into the lives of Christians in the business world. No one is to check his or her faith at the office, factory, or shop door. Ethics in business must include conducting business in every aspect as though God matters despite how others act and think.

when he prayed, "Father, if you are willing, take this cup away from me; yet not my will, but yours be done" (Luke 22:42). Jesus expects his disciples to do no less. James reinforced that every thought that a Christian has must first be filtered by God's will.

To think as though God does not matter is a form of self-reliant pride. Verse 16 calls it "evil" and "boasting." Note James 1:9, "The brother in humble circumstances ought to take pride in his high position." "Humble circumstances" often lead one to a more trusting faith (the point of chapter 1). Boasting of what we can accomplish aside from God's provision is simple pride in self.

James then mentioned the sin of omission (James 4:17). Sin is more than the wrong things that are done. The sins of omission are those good things left undone. Failing to look for God's will is sin. Knowing the will of God and failing to do it is also a sin. Further, Christians are guilty of sinning when we do not care about the real hardship and needs of those around us. Even more so, once aware of the needs, we are certainly guilty of sinning by not serving God or the needs before us.

Holding Possessions as Though God Doesn't Matter (5:1–3)

The Bible has a lot to say about wealth. Wealth in and of itself is not a bad thing, but its close association with many bad things ought to be a warning to Christians. Verses 1–3 are written in reverse order of sin, judgment, and finally the consequence of judgment. Hoarding wealth is listed as a sin (5:3). Verse 2 describes the judgment as the loss of that wealth. Verse 1 describes the consequence of judgment: weeping, wailing, and misery.

Hoarding wealth is a symptom of several sins. Hoarding wealth demonstrates trust in self instead of trust in God. Jesus' parable about the talents demonstrates that God gives wealth to us to be used for his purposes (Luke 19:12–27). Second, hoarding wealth shows we do not care about God's purposes and are just interested in ourselves; thus, it is a sin of omission. Third, it also reveals a lack of love and concern for those in need. Most of all, hoarding wealth is the outward display of greed, which is one of the symptoms of ungodliness (2 Timothy 3:2–5). Ultimately, hoarding wealth does no good, like someone running around gathering jewelry on the Titanic. Human wealth has no eternal value. On the other hand, what could be accomplished with wealth might have great eternal worth.

The judgment (James 5:2) is fitting and further illustrates the illusion of wealth. What seems like great security (gold) will not be lasting. Wealth will rot. Even that which seems incorruptible (gold) will corrode and crumble away. Stock market crashes, personal bankruptcies, foreclosures, and layoffs are examples of sudden unplanned and often unforeseen loss. In these situations, it certainly may seem like the gold has corroded. Security is found in God, not in the accumulation of wealth.

Verse 1 reveals the heart of the hoarder. Misery comes in the form of weeping and wailing, which comes from one of two things: (1) deep grief of loss showing that the person's trust was completely in the possessions; or (2) a repentant heart suffering through the shock of misplaced trust and loss. Sadly, the reality is that there will be people on Judgment Day—or before—who realize that their wealth ultimately amounts to nothing.

Hoarding wealth as though God does not matter will prove to be its own demise. God does matter. We are only stewards of what God provides for us and allows us to handle. If we prove faithful or not, God will notice.

Treating Others as Though God Doesn't Matter (5:4–6)

How we treat people matters to God. People are more valuable to God than money; yet some people see others as just another resource to help them build wealth. We have already seen that wealth will not last forever, but our actions toward others will. Verses 4–6 give two examples of how

DEO VOLENTE

The Latin phrase *Deo Volente* (*God willing*) has long been used in the Christian world. The use of such a phrase carries religious overtones, but its careless use amounts to breaking the third commandment of misusing the Lord's name. It is vain to say we are doing something according to God's will while never actually seeking to know or do God's will.

people treat others as though God does not matter: direct and indirect injustices.

Direct injustices include unfair employment, political, and judicial practices. Verse 4 describes an employer withholding wages but represents a larger issue of those crying out for fair employment practices. The most obvious meaning is the employer who cheats the employee out of a well-deserved payment. Verse 6 condemns the abuses of the courts.

Many Christians may easily dismiss these verses as not applying to them, but we may be guilty of treating others poorly if we comply with any form of unfairness and injustice. We may also be guilty if we turn a deaf ear when we hear the cries of those enduring injustice. We need to be serious about how our lives affect the world. Do we benefit in any way because of abusive labor practices in other parts of the world? Do we sit back and allow the innocent to be treated unfairly?

Indirect injustice as seen in the heartlessness of the wealthy (5:5), along with the hoarding of wealth (5:3), and an insensitive attitude toward the cries of the hurting (5:4), reveals a viewpoint inconsistent with the love of God. In 1 John, John wrote that this heartlessness may be a test exposing whether an individual has the love of God, "We know that we have passed from death to life, because we love our brothers. Anyone who does not love remains in death. . . . If anyone has material possessions and sees his brother in need but has no pity on him, how can the love of God be in him?" (1 John 3:14, 17). An obvious evidence indicating this type of injustice is more concern for personal luxury and self-indulgence than for those crying out in need. The result of such living ("fattened yourselves in the day of slaughter," 5:5) will be the Day of Judgment, in which such heartlessness will bring condemnation.

Implications and Actions

It is assumed that every Christian would have the same answer if asked whether God matters, *Of course God matters*. However, actions speak louder than words. Real faith in action is living every moment as though God matters. Being a disciple of Jesus means that how we think, what we do, what we have, what we share, and how we treat others matters to God. Think about the week to come. How will you live differently knowing that God matters?

QUESTIONS

1. Did you consider God when you took the job you currently have? Do you consider God's will when making plans at work or home? Or do you make plans and then later ask God to bless them?

2. Does God regularly cross your mind or only at church? Do you think more like your Christian friends or more like your non-Christian friends?

3. Are you obsessed with accumulating wealth? Do you check your balances too often? Does your wealth have a purpose, or are you accumulating wealth just to have it? Are you hoarding wealth and not using any to serve God? What good have you done with money in the last year, or in the last five years?

4. Do you treat people well? Do you consider the plight of others less fortunate? Is it easy for you to overlook the distress of others? Have you knowingly ignored helping someone because it would not benefit you?

NOTES

1. Unless otherwise indicated, all Scripture quotations in lessons 5–6 are from the New International Version.

Living Faith in Christian Community

FOCAL TEXT
James 5:7–20

BACKGROUND
James 5:7–20

MAIN IDEA
A true Christian community is not just another group of people but is characterized by qualities of authentic Christian faith.

QUESTIONS TO EXPLORE
What qualities should we aim for in true Christian community? How are we doing?

STUDY AIM
To evaluate my church and Bible study group by the qualities of congregational life James encouraged

QUICK READ
Christians come together to form communities of faith, providing a place for personal spiritual growth and mutually beneficial fellowship.

In the movie *Cast Away*, the character played by Tom Hanks has to learn to live alone and isolated after an airplane crash and reveals that it is not a good thing to be left alone on an island. His need for community is so real that he uses a volleyball named *Wilson* to fulfill his need for companionship.

Likewise, Christians are meant to be in relationship with one another. Real living faith is cultivated and maintained in a healthy community. Faith will not survive well if it is isolated on a spiritual island. James explored four areas in which a Christian community cultivates a living faith: by developing patience, by being a place of integrity, by maintaining an enriched prayer life, and by protecting one another.

JAMES 5:7–20

7 Be patient, then, brothers, until the Lord's coming. See how the farmer waits for the land to yield its valuable crop and how patient he is for the autumn and spring rains. 8 You too, be patient and stand firm, because the Lord's coming is near. 9 Don't grumble against each other, brothers, or you will be judged. The Judge is standing at the door! 10 Brothers, as an example of patience in the face of suffering, take the prophets who spoke in the name of the Lord. 11 As you know, we consider blessed those who have persevered. You have heard of Job's perseverance and have seen what the Lord finally brought about. The Lord is full of compassion and mercy. 12 Above all, my brothers, do not swear—not by heaven or by earth or by anything else. Let your "Yes" be yes, and your "No," no, or you will be condemned. 13 Is any one of you in trouble? He should pray. Is anyone happy? Let him sing songs of praise. 14 Is any one of you sick? He should call the elders of the church to pray over him and anoint him with oil in the name of the Lord. 15 And the prayer offered in faith will make the sick person well; the Lord will raise him up. If he has sinned, he will be forgiven. 16 Therefore confess your sins to each other and pray for each other so that you may be healed. The prayer of a righteous man is powerful and effective. 17 Elijah was a man just like us. He prayed earnestly that it would not rain, and it did not rain on the land for three and a half

years. [18] Again he prayed, and the heavens gave rain, and the earth produced its crops. [19] My brothers, if one of you should wander from the truth and someone should bring him back, [20] remember this: Whoever turns a sinner from the error of his way will save him from death and cover over a multitude of sins.

A Patient Community (5:7–11)

We live in an impatient world. We have little patience for what others do or for what we are waiting on, even as Christians. Developing patience is one benefit of living in a Christian community. Each of these five verses examines an area of patience that every Christian can nurture with a focus on God while relying on God's power.

To begin with, patience within a living faith is not just sitting idly, waiting for the world to pass by, but rather is an optimistic expectation. James provided two examples: the Lord's coming and a farmer waiting on his crop (5:7). In both cases, patience is tied to hope and anticipation. The Lord will return, and the crops should come. An expectant patience is the realization and acceptance of our limits while trusting in God to provide that which we anticipate, demonstrating patience with a purpose.

Patience within the Christian community is a *steadfast* patience. "Be patient and stand firm" (5:8) is a command to be resolute and strong in a world of sin and weakness. Knowing that the Lord will come again allows Christians to maintain a fortified faith that will stand the test of time, demonstrating patience with determination.

We are commanded to be patient with one another (5:9). Ironically, we tend to lose our patience with those who are closest to us: our spouses, children, siblings, friends, and co-workers we see daily; and people within our Christian communities. We do "grumble against each other," showing our lack of patience despite what the Bible teaches. James offered a sober caution. As sure as "the Lord's coming is near" (5:8), "the Judge is standing at the door" (5:9) for those who are grumbling against one another. Let us be kind to one another, demonstrating patience with love.

Patience is also the ability to handle suffering. The prophets in the Old Testament suffered for many reasons (5:10)—at the hands of an evil king (Elijah), because of an enemy nation (Daniel), because of the rejection of the people of that day (Jeremiah), and as an example of God's judgment (Ezekiel), to name a few. Having faith does not exempt anyone from the problems of this world, but faith gives us a way of handling problems, demonstrating patience under fire.

Endurance is the last aspect of patience that is mentioned. "Perseverance" (*hypomone*) or "endurance" (NASB, NRSV) is used (5:11) instead of "patience" (*makrothymeo*, 5:7, 8, 10), implying a slight difference in meaning. "Patience" basically refers to *waiting*. The surrounding text in 5:7, 8, 10 helps develop the fuller meaning of the additional aspects of "patience." "Perseverance" (NIV) or "endurance" (NASB, NRSV) is from *hypomone*, which means *patience with fortification*. Living faith provides the ability to endure even in the most trying of circumstances, demonstrating patience with lasting strength.

Are you a patient person? Are you helping others to develop Christ-focused endurance? Does your church or small group nurture patience, or do you assemble to grumble? Let us be sure that our Christian communities are patient communities.

A Community of Integrity (5:12)

James 5:12 refers to the teaching of Jesus in Matthew 5:33–37. Christians must be people of integrity, especially here in what they say. This is the third mention of the tongue in James, emphasizing that what we say is important to God. Earlier, James warned believers to control their tongues (James 1:26) and to let them be instruments of praise rather than of cursing (3:7–12). In the context of community, we must be truthful with one another. The prohibition against swearing by heaven or earth stresses that Christians should not have to swear by anything. They should be credible enough to be taken at their initial word.

A student in my fifth-grade class would always say, "I swear on a stack of Bibles," when he told us anything so that we would believe him. The problem was that no one would ever believe anything he said, even with a stack of Bibles nearby. Simple honesty is all a Christian ever needs. As a part of the community of faith, Christians must be honest with one another. The Christian community as a whole must demonstrate the same integrity to the rest of the world in order to be trustworthy, without having to have a stack of Bibles in hand.

Are you a person of integrity? Do you feel that your church is a community of integrity in which everyone is honest and sincere with each other, or is it a place where two-faced insincerity exists?

A Community of Prayer (5:13–18)

The church must be a community of prayer. This section reveals the place, privilege, and power of prayer in the community. Prayer's place in the church is central in time and importance. Praying for one another is always appropriate. We are to pray for one another whether suffering, sick, or ready to praise God.

The privilege that Christians have in praying for one another is great. One of the simplest but most profound moments that Christians can share occurs when one prays for another by name while in the person's presence. In that moment each person in the prayer is joining in a common thought and spirit along with God himself.

The anointing of oil has both practical and pastoral meaning. There were no drugstores in the first century. Many medicines were regional or home remedies utilizing simple ingredients with olive oil or honey as a base. These had practical applications of being a mild antiseptic, sealing off a wound, or comforting damaged tissues, similarly to the

---

THE PERSEVERANCE OF JOB

Job is a wonderful story of *perseverance*, not *patience* as we generally understand the word. Despite popular opinion, Job was not a patient person. Some translators of James 5:11 have contributed to this misunderstanding by using *patience* instead of *endurance* or *perseverance*. Instead of being patient, Job had a tremendous long-suffering endurance. He questioned God. He wondered whether life was worth living. At times he wished he was dead, but at the end of it all he endured and revealed a living faith that was tested as genuine. Job provides an example for all of us of lasting strength in the most difficult times.

use of lotions today. Of course, modern advances have improved care significantly, and modern medicines should be used in the same way oil was used then. However, the pastoral meaning of anointing with oil was strong then and carries the same meaning today.

A Christian community should be a place of love, care, and concern. Anointing with oil is a caring pastoral act of concern for the individual who is sick. Gathering the elders of the church around the person is the perfect example of being a community of prayer. Imagine the leaders of any church joining hands, unified in spirit, caring for an individual, approaching our Father in heaven. What an act of fellowship, ministry, and worship! It would be hard for a church genuinely doing so to squabble about the non-essential things that tend to divide.

Another aspect of the privilege of prayer is confessing sins to each other. Confession builds a tension of trust, vulnerability, accountability, and confidence in each other. It is a privilege to be allowed into the lives of others to such a depth. We overlook (or even abuse) that privilege when we thoughtlessly ramble through a prayer request list. Each name represents an individual or a family hurting, struggling, worrying, grieving, or dealing with issues central to their lives. Understanding

THE PRAYER OF ELIJAH

Elijah was a prophet who spoke on behalf of God against Ahab, the wicked King of Israel, and his wife Jezebel (see 1 Kings 17—18). In communion with God, he announced a three-year drought in the land of Israel. Elijah went north out of Israel until God told him it was time to end the drought and called Elijah back to Israel.

Even though God could have ended the drought without Elijah, God chose not to. Elijah was the greatest known righteous man in the land. James used this example to illustrate that we must have high integrity and righteousness in order to be fit to be a useful instrument for God.

The rains came after Elijah challenged 450 false prophets and defeated them in a test of faith. The testament to Elijah's faith is found at the end of Elijah's part of the test, "In a little while, the heavens grew black with clouds and wind; there was a heavy rain" (1 Kings 18:45, NRSV).

LESSON 6: Living Faith in Christian Community

those personal needs can help drive the members of a Christian community toward a richer living faith.

The most important aspect of prayer is its power. James 5:16b is one of the classic Scriptures regarding prayer in the Bible, "The effective prayer of a righteous man can accomplish much" (NASB). The first two parts of this verse reveal why prayer seems so ineffective to many people. It begins by stating that the prayer must be "effective" (intense). Many Christians should honestly examine their prayer lives to see whether they have intensity. Examine how often you pray meaningful prayers in a day (or in a week). Examine the amount of time you devote to prayer each time you pray. Is it less than twenty minutes? Is it less than five minutes? Intense prayer implies a commitment of time and heart, devotion to God, and concern about the matters at hand.

The second part of the verse indicates that powerful praying comes from righteous people. A religion professor of mine said that although this verse is true, you might have to ask forty people to pray for you to be sure you get at least one righteous person! All jokes aside, the point that the verse (and the surrounding ones) is making is that powerful prayer is found in the context of a sincere faith and supported by a life of integrity and endurance until the end, in contrast to the mediocre prayer life of a haphazardly obedient Christian.

A Community that Protects One Another (5:19–20)

Compare James's words in James 5:19–20 with Paul's words in Galatians 6:1, "Brothers, if someone is caught in a sin, you who are spiritual should restore him gently. But watch yourself, or you also may be tempted." Another privilege and responsibility of being in community is that we care about what happens to one another in a redemptive manner, thereby protecting one another, which can only be done if we are sensitive enough to notice one another's spiritual lives. We should know when we can help one another and when a Christian brother or sister "wanders from the truth" so that we can bring him or her back. We are privileged to be a useful tool for God in helping others.

Although God saves sinners, James reminds us that "whoever turns a sinner from the error of his way will save him from death and cover over a multitude of sins" (James 5:20). The church as a community is responsible for intervening in a life headed the wrong direction, thereby turning the "sinner" from a destructive course, a course that leads to death, either in this life or the life to come. The community is not saving the sinner but assisting in directing him or her to the one true Savior.

Implications and Actions

Beyond developing a personal living faith, Christians gather together as a community, having the privilege and the responsibility of investing our lives in one another. Each individual affects the community, and in return as a whole the community affects each believer. We learn patience with one another and in the face of the things of this world. We should demonstrate lives of integrity, both as the Christian community and in our own private lives. We must develop effective prayer lives based on obedient lives. We ought to protect one another and as a community guide each person to reject a path of sin and follow the way of righteousness. Together each of us grows stronger in our faith as we invest in one another as a living community.

QUESTIONS

1. Do you consider yourself to be a part of a Christian community? Or are you an isolated Christian? How can you foster kinship with other Christians?

2. Are you a patient person? What makes you impatient with other people? As a whole, is your church or Bible study group a patient community? How can we all be more patient as a community?

3. Does your *yes* always mean *yes*? Are you honest with people in your life? What do you try to hide from others, from God, or even from yourself? How can we be a community of integrity?

4. Do you want a more effective prayer life? Would you say you are consistent in your personal prayer life? Is it strong, passionate, and trusting? Or is it mediocre, inconsistent, and infrequent? Are you willing to make a covenant with others to develop an effective prayer community?

5. Are you interested in protecting other Christians? How can your group become a protecting community?

The Letters of John: Tests of Genuine Christianity

Profound Thoughts in Simple Language

The Letters of John contain profound thoughts couched in simple language. First John, in fact, is written so simply that it generally is the first biblical book that a person learning to read the Greek New Testament begins to translate. The ideas, though, are as profound as the words are simple. Love, obedience, faith—no words could be simpler or more profound at the same time.

Even though the thoughts are profound and sometimes difficult to understand, we'll find them to be clear enough, so clear that over and over again we'll be asked to face up to an important question: *Is our Christian faith truly genuine?* In this sense, 1 John, perhaps surprisingly, deals with a concern somewhat similar to that of the Book of James but approaches the concern in a different manner.

The Structure of 1 John

One of the factors that makes understanding and applying 1 John a challenge is its structure. Our culture teaches us to expect a piece of literature, including the Bible, to deal with one subject and then move to the next and the next. We won't find that pattern in 1 John. Instead, what we'll find is that John often deals briefly with a topic, moves to the next and the next, and then weaves all of them together. Perhaps that's why a book on the Letters of John by Baptist theology professor and Bible commentator Bill Hendricks is subtitled "Tapestries of Truth."[1]

In an older commentary on 1 John,[2] Robert Law stated that 1 John has a *spiral* structure, a view with which many later commentators agree. He went on to say that the emphasis of the letter is on setting forth, over and over, these tests of Christianity: righteousness, love, and belief.[3] However, the thoughts of 1 John don't just go round and round as they spiral upward. Rather the themes are intertwined as they spiral round and round and up and up. So perhaps a more specific way of picturing the structure is to call it a *triple helix*. What's a *triple helix*? The definition is not as complicated as it might sound. Just picture three different-colored strands of thick thread entwined or braided together. That's similar to a triple helix, and that image illustrates the structure of 1 John. The three main topics of obedience (or righteousness), love for God and others, and belief in Jesus as human as well as divine are all entwined and appear over and over.

Like a good teacher, John continually comes back to these essential themes so we won't miss them. John won't let us be done with any of these crucial strands of meaning. He keeps on coming back to them—to love, obedience, and belief—so we'll be sure to get them and do something about them.

THE LETTERS OF JOHN: TESTS OF GENUINE CHRISTIANITY

Lesson 7	Centering Life on the Word of Life	1 John 1:1—2:2
Lesson 8	Knowing We Know God	1 John 2:3–27
Lesson 9	Facing the Future with Confidence	1 John 2:28—3:10
Lesson 10	Loving to the *N*th Degree	1 John 3:11–18; 4:7–12, 19–21
Lesson 11	Believing in God's Divine-Human Son	1 John 4:1–6, 13–16a
Lesson 12	Living By the Logic of Love and Faith	1 John 5
Lesson 13	Support God's Work Generously and Wisely	2 John 1–2, 7–11; 3 John 1–11

Additional Resources for Studying 1, 2, 3 John[4]

C. Clifton Black. "The First, Second, and Third Letters of John." *New Interpreter's Bible*. Volume XII. Nashville: Abingdon Press, 1998.

Raymond E. Brown. *The Epistles of John*. The Anchor Bible. Volume 30. Garden City, New York: Doubleday & Company, Inc., 1982.

R. Alan Culpepper. *1 John, 2 John, 3 John.* Knox Preaching Guides. Atlanta: John Knox Press, 1985.

William L. Hendricks. *The Letters of John.* Nashville, Tennessee: Convention Press, 1970.

Craig S. Keener. *IVP Bible Background Commentary: New Testament.* Downers Grove, Illinois: InterVarsity Press, 1993.

I. Howard Marshall. *The Epistles of John.* The New International Commentary on the New Testament. Grand Rapids, Michigan: William B. Eerdmans Publishing Company, 1978.

Edward A. McDowell. "1–2–3 John." *The Broadman Bible Commentary.* Volume 12. Nashville: Broadman Press, 1972.

Earl F. Palmer. *1, 2, 3 John, Revelation.* The Communicator's Commentary. Waco, Texas: Word Books, Publisher, 1982.

A.T. Robertson. *Word Pictures in the New Testament.* Volume VI. Nashville, Tennessee: Broadman Press, 1933.

Stephen S. Smalley. *1, 2, 3 John.* Word Biblical Commentary. Volume 51. Waco, Texas: Word Books, Publisher, 1984.

D. Moody Smith. *First, Second, and Third John.* Interpretation: A Bible Commentary for Preaching and Teaching. Louisville: John Knox Press, 1991.

John R. W. Stott. *The Letters of John.* Revised edition. Tyndale New Testament Commentaries. Grand Rapids, Michigan: William B. Eerdmans Publishing Company, 1988.

NOTES

1. William L. Hendricks, *The Letters of John* (Nashville, Tennessee: Convention Press, 1970).

2. Robert Law, *The Tests of Life, a Study of the First Epistle of St. John*, 3rd ed. (Edinburgh: T & T Clark, 1909,1913). See http://www.archive.org/details/thetestsoflifeas00lawruoft. Accessed 12/4/09.

3. Law, *The Tests of Life*, chapter 1.

4. Listing a book does not imply full agreement by the writers or BAPTISTWAY PRESS® with all of its comments.

FOCAL TEXT
1 John 1:1—2:2

BACKGROUND
1 John 1:1—2:2

MAIN IDEA
Receiving the life made
available to us in God's
sending his Son opens the
way for us to live our lives
in fellowship with him.

QUESTION TO EXPLORE
What does having our lives
centered on Christ mean?

STUDY AIM
To consider whether
and how my life is truly
centered on Christ

QUICK READ
A vital, life-changing
encounter with God in Jesus
Christ leads to a lifestyle
that leaves sin behind and
brings fellowship with God
and others. But when sin
does occur, confession brings
forgiveness through Christ.

LESSON SEVEN
Centering Life on the Word of Life

During the 2009–2010 football season, three champion college quarterbacks testified to their Christian faith (Colt McCoy, Sam Bradford, Tim Tebow). During the same time frame, Drew Brees, quarterback of the New Orleans Saints in their drive to the professional football championship in the Super Bowl, also testified of his Christian faith.[1] Why do such testimonies often have an impact?

Sports fans of all ages respect what these young men can do athletically. This respect gives entrée for their testimonies to gain a hearing. Testimony based on personal experience can be powerful and hard to deny.

But wait. You may not be a sports hero or be otherwise famous, but your Christian testimony is valuable, too, because it is based on your own personal experience. In fact, your testimony may pack more punch than you realize. This passage from 1 John is powerful for many reasons, but one certainly is that it is testimony based on personal experience.[2]

1 JOHN 1:1–10

[1] We declare to you what was from the beginning, what we have heard, what we have seen with our eyes, what we have looked at and touched with our hands, concerning the word of life— [2] this life was revealed, and we have seen it and testify to it, and declare to you the eternal life that was with the Father and was revealed to us— [3] we declare to you what we have seen and heard so that you also may have fellowship with us; and truly our fellowship is with the Father and with his Son Jesus Christ. [4] We are writing these things so that our joy may be complete.

[5] This is the message we have heard from him and proclaim to you, that God is light and in him there is no darkness at all. [6] If we say that we have fellowship with him while we are walking in darkness, we lie and do not do what is true; [7] but if we walk in the light as he himself is in the light, we have fellowship with one another, and the blood of Jesus his Son cleanses us from all sin. [8] If we say that we have no sin, we deceive ourselves, and the truth is not in us. [9] If we confess our sins, he who is faithful and just will forgive us our sins and cleanse us from all unrighteousness. [10] If

we say that we have not sinned, we make him a liar, and his word is not in us.

1 JOHN 2:1–2

[1] My little children, I am writing these things to you so that you may not sin. But if anyone does sin, we have an advocate with the Father, Jesus Christ the righteous; [2] and he is the atoning sacrifice for our sins, and not for ours only but also for the sins of the whole world.

A Genuine Experience with Christ (1:1–4)

"From the beginning"—John chose his inspired words with care. Each word counts. Compare these verses with the opening verses of the Gospel of John. Then look at the first several verses of Genesis. You can see in these comparisons that John connected Christ with creation. In the Gospel of John, the Word was present and active in that creation. Here John said that they had experienced that same God in Christ.

"What we have heard, what we have seen with our eyes" connects John's experience with the incarnation of Jesus and beyond that to God's forming of the world! John asserted that he wrote from personal experience. His testimony was based on his own encounters with the Lord. The word "we" points to a community of friends who had shared these experiences and were continuing to witness to these experiences. Christians today have their own encounters with Christ to experience and a community in which to both experience them and testify about them.

"What we have looked at and touched with our hands"—With this phrase and the preceding one about hearing, three of our five senses are mentioned. The disciples experienced Jesus in his humanity. They heard his teachings; they saw him personally; they rubbed shoulders with him. In short, Jesus came into their world and influenced them more than anyone or anything else in life. The experiences of the first disciples with Jesus were real and physical. Jesus was not a god in disguise, as many Greek myths told of their gods, but he was genuinely a man. Fully human as well as fully divine! Jesus' disciples centered their lives on him.

"Concerning the word of life" contains two important words—"word" and "life." "Word" relates first to the *word* God spoke at creation: "And God said" (Genesis 1:3, 6, 9, 11, 14, 20, 24, 26, 29). God created by speaking, by the *word*. Later, in the prophets, we repeatedly read that "the word of the Lord came to [a prophet] saying. . . " (for example, Jonah 1:1). Then John's Gospel speaks of "the Word" being at the beginning and now come in the flesh (John 1:1, 14). In 1 John, we find that same *word* of the Lord associated with life.

For John, "life" is more than breathing and existing. The life Jesus gives is rich and full. God's life is abundant life, purposeful life, and transforming life. That life had been "revealed" to them in the person of Jesus Christ (1 John 1:2). The writer had found that life in his own personal meeting with Jesus.

"So that you also may have fellowship with us"—This is the reason for John's writing. "Fellowship" was a far deeper thing for early Christians than we usually feel today. That *koinonia* (Greek word for "fellowship"; see small article, "Fellowship") was a closeness developed out of common experiences "with the Father and with his Son Jesus Christ." We encounter Christ, and through Christ we meet the Father. Then we share common fellowship with all others who know him. John also tells us that Jesus' relation to God is as a son to a father. We thus become a fellowship of brothers and sisters in Christ. We don't call each other *brother* or *sister* much anymore, as previous generations of Christians did, but we are indeed the family of God—a family in fellowship with God and one another.

Fellowship brings joy. John said he wrote so his and his friends' "joy may be complete" (1:4). In sports, games have winners and losers, those in joy and those in despair. Competition makes it so. But the Christian life is not so limited. There's plenty of joy to go around. Proclaiming the message spreads that joy as people accept it. Have you found joy in sharing Christ?

These first four verses read as if John was so excited that he was excitedly pouring out his memories and thoughts in a gush of words. As he did, he mentioned several themes that will reappear in the following chapters. Watch for them as you continue to study.

The Message: God Is Light (1:5–7)

Once again, John linked his thoughts with Genesis and the Gospel of John when he wrote, "God is light." In creation, God's first word of command was, "Let there be light" (Gen. 1:3). John's Gospel says Jesus' "life was the light of men" (John 1:4, NIV). The contrast between light and darkness resonates in every culture. For John, the richness of life in Christ shines a beacon on life's pathway. That life reveals right and wrong, good and evil, sin and righteousness. The Christian life compared to life without Christ is as different as light is from darkness. Now in 1 John, we read that "God is light and in him there is no darkness at all" (1 John 1:5). God is the source of all that is good, moral, and just. God has no evil in his nature or in his behavior.

Strong, blunt words come next. Because of the nature of God as "light," to claim fellowship with God while walking in "darkness" means "we lie and do not do what is true." In the Bible, truth is something one does as much as something one believes. Faith and works are not separate. Faith drives works. Fellowship with God includes obedience to God. To claim one without the other is to lie.

On the other hand, when we live uprightly and righteously as God is upright and righteous, we have fellowship, not only with God, but with one another. Such a life bears witness to God's presence in us. Such a life is also life in community, to be lived in fellowship with one another.

FELLOWSHIP

Fellowship is the bond created when a person unites with Christ. The relationship with God results in a connection to other members of God's family, fellow Christians. Fellowship means unity, sharing, participation. Just as teammates depend on one another in athletics, so does the church rely on a common love and support among her members. That bond is the glue that holds the church together. Fellowship is always mutual. Each must give and also receive trust and affection for fellowship to happen. Fellowship with God includes allowing God to mold us in the likeness of Christ.

When Sin Comes (1:8—2:2)

Even as Christians who normally walk in the light, we do sin. John claimed starkly that we lie if we deny our sin. We may, in fact, be deceiving ourselves.

Psychologists talk of *projection*, the tendency to project our thoughts, including our faults, to another. We thus proclaim the other person is guilty but not ourselves. By pointing the finger, we think we don't have to look at our own faults. Jesus pointed out the neglect of logs in one's own eye while obsessing over the splinter in another's eye (Matt. 7:3–5).

As pastor and counselor, I have used 1 John 1:9 more than any other Scripture throughout my forty-five years of ministry. I have encountered many people who could not escape the feelings of guilt for actions from many years ago. If you are one who carries that burden, this verse is for you. Claim it. "If we confess our sins, he . . . will forgive us our sins. . . ." Did you confess your sins? (Some will repeatedly say, *Yes*.) Then God forgave you the first time you asked. That sin is gone. If God forgave it, you have no right to hang on to it. Are you more righteous than God?

"Cleanse us from all unrighteousness"—Not only does God forgive us, but God also continues to cleanse us from all unrighteousness. The cleansing is part of the forgiveness. Parents sometimes chastise a child for playing in the mud, and yet at their best they lovingly help the child take off dirty clothes and get clean again in the tub. The incident is forgotten the next day.

GROWING IN THE CHRISTIAN LIFE:

- Review your Christian experience. What have you seen, heard, and felt?
- Strengthen your fellowship. Reach out to other church members you don't know well.
- Accept God's forgiveness for past sins, mistakes, and faults.
- Face up to character flaws that persist. Open them to the Spirit for change!

Chapter divisions were not entered into the text until long after the New Testament was written, and 1 John 2:1–2 are part of this same discussion from chapter 1. Note the affectionate expression in 2:1, "My little children." These words indicate that John and this letter's first readers enjoyed a close, loving, almost parental relationship.

The writer wanted his readers to avoid sin. But if and when someone did sin, he let them know that they had an "advocate" to intercede for them "with the Father" (1 John 2:1). That advocate is Jesus Christ, whose blood was cleansing them from all sin (1:7, 9). The word "advocate" means *one who stands beside you.* Jesus used the same word of the Holy Spirit in John 16:7.

John also stated that Jesus is the "atoning sacrifice for our sins" (2:2). In the ancient system, one paid for sins by sacrificing various animals, small or large, depending on how serious the sin was. When Jesus died on the cross, he paid for all sins. Readers of John's day would immediately have understood, for they likely had sacrificed or at least witnessed sacrifice. For us, too, Jesus "is the atoning sacrifice for our sins." He has set us free for our sins and guilt.

Applying the Lesson to Life

Use these four questions to review 1 John 1:1—2:2 and apply it to your life:

- First, do you personally understand the teachings of 1 John 1:1–4 about the nature of God and Christ?
- Second, do you grasp how walking "in the light" reflects the character of God?
- Third, do you hear the call to confront sin, admit it to yourself, and confess it to God so you can receive forgiveness and cleansing?
- Finally, do you have excitement and joy in your life because of your experiences with a living God?

QUESTIONS

1. How close is your fellowship with God?

2. How well does your life and character reflect the character of Christ?

3. Which verse in this passage speaks most pointedly about dealing with guilt? Have you received the forgiveness God offers you? Will you?

4. What do these verses say about denying sin and flaws in one's behavior?

NOTES

1. See www.youtube.com/watch?v=t0buCfbFuHw. Accessed 4/21/10.

2. Unless otherwise indicated, all Scripture quotations in lessons 7–8 are from the New Revised Standard Version Bible.

LESSON EIGHT
Knowing We Know God

FOCAL TEXT
1 John 2:3–27

BACKGROUND
1 John 2:3–27

MAIN IDEA
Whether one truly knows God can be tested by whether one obeys God, relates in love to others, and believes Jesus truly is the Christ.

QUESTION TO EXPLORE
How can we know we know God?

STUDY AIM
To consider whether I truly know God

QUICK READ
Three basic tests demonstrate whether you know God. The first test looks for your obedience to God's truth. The second test relates to whether you love others. The third test explores whether you confess that Jesus truly is the Christ.

"There are too many hypocrites in your church," the man said to me. "I rub shoulders with them every week. I see them doing things I would not do, and I don't claim to be a Christian." I explained to him that the church was not a museum for saints, but a hospital for sick souls. Nevertheless, he had a point. Can people tell you are a believer by your behavior?

1 JOHN 2:3–27

3 Now by this we may be sure that we know him, if we obey his commandments. 4 Whoever says, "I have come to know him," but does not obey his commandments, is a liar, and in such a person the truth does not exist; 5 but whoever obeys his word, truly in this person the love of God has reached perfection. By this we may be sure that we are in him: 6 whoever says, "I abide in him," ought to walk just as he walked.

7 Beloved, I am writing you no new commandment, but an old commandment that you have had from the beginning; the old commandment is the word that you have heard. 8 Yet I am writing you a new commandment that is true in him and in you, because the darkness is passing away and the true light is already shining. 9 Whoever says, "I am in the light," while hating a brother or sister, is still in the darkness. 10 Whoever loves a brother or sister lives in the light, and in such a person there is no cause for stumbling. 11 But whoever hates another believer is in the darkness, walks in the darkness, and does not know the way to go, because the darkness has brought on blindness.

12 I am writing to you, little children,
    because your sins are forgiven on account of his name.
13 I am writing to you, fathers,
    because you know him who is from the beginning.
I am writing to you, young people,
    because you have conquered the evil one.
14 I write to you, children,
    because you know the Father.
I write to you, fathers,
    because you know him who is from the beginning.

I write to you, young people,
    because you are strong
    and the word of God abides in you,
and you have overcome the evil one.

[15] Do not love the world or the things in the world. The love of the Father is not in those who love the world; [16] for all that is in the world—the desire of the flesh, the desire of the eyes, the pride in riches—comes not from the Father but from the world. [17] And the world and its desire are passing away, but those who do the will of God live forever.

[18] Children, it is the last hour! As you have heard that antichrist is coming, so now many antichrists have come. From this we know that it is the last hour. [19] They went out from us, but they did not belong to us; for if they had belonged to us, they would have remained with us. But by going out they made it plain that none of them belongs to us. [20] But you have been anointed by the Holy One, and all of you have knowledge. [21] I write to you, not because you do not know the truth, but because you know it, and you know that no lie comes from the truth. [22] Who is the liar but the one who denies that Jesus is the Christ? This is the antichrist, the one who denies the Father and the Son. [23] No one who denies the Son has the Father; everyone who confesses the Son has the Father also. [24] Let what you heard from the beginning abide in you. If what you heard from the beginning abides in you, then you will abide in the Son and in the Father. [25] And this is what he has promised us, eternal life.

[26] I write these things to you concerning those who would deceive you. [27] As for you, the anointing that you received from him abides in you, and so you do not need anyone to teach you. But as his anointing teaches you about all things, and is true and is not a lie, and just as it has taught you, abide in him.

Walking in Obedience (2:3–6)

John had little use for people who claimed with their words that they were Christians but did not live out their profession of Christ in real life.

For John, faith and works were not separate. If you want to be sure you know Jesus, then "obey his commandments." If you claim to belong to Christ and do not obey, John says you are a liar. He goes further and says for such a person truth does not exist. Truth is not only something to be believed, but truth is also something to be done.

On the other hand, for those who obey, their obedience shows their love for the Lord has reached "perfection" (1 John 2:5). Biblical perfection does not so much mean *without flaw* as it means *maturity* or *completion*. Love leads to obedience. When you obey, you are demonstrating that your love is causing you to grow into maturity as a Christian. John repeated himself for emphasis, saying that if we claim to abide in Jesus, we must walk the walk Jesus taught us (2:6).

A New Commandment (2:7–11)

John next stated he was telling his readers nothing new. He was repeating "an old commandment" (2:7). To which commandment was he referring? Possibly it was Deuteronomy 6:4–5, the watchword of Israel. "Hear, O Israel: The LORD is our God, the LORD alone. You shall love the LORD your God with all your heart, and with all your soul, and with all your might." These verses affirm the oneness of God and the demand for total love of the Lord. Jesus himself called this the greatest

KNOWLEDGE

In the Bible, *knowledge* almost always means *knowing from experience*, not merely *head knowledge*. To know Christ means to experience him, commit to him, and allow his Spirit within your life.

In the Greek world, there were many mystery religions. In many of these religions, salvation was believed to come through an initiation in which one received secret knowledge. We call these groups *Gnostics* from the Greek word for *knowledge*. Many groups of Gnostics sought to inject their ideas into the early church. This contest lies behind much of the New Testament. Most likely John's discussion of knowledge in 1 John 2:18–27 was intended to tell them not to listen to self-appointed teachers who put out false doctrine.

commandment, and he added a second, the love of neighbor as oneself. That too is from the Old Testament (Leviticus 19:18). The old commandment, John said, "is the word that you have heard."

Then John wrote about "a new commandment that is true in him and in you" (1 John 2:8). Again, we wonder what that word might be. Many believe John was referring to John 13:34, where Jesus commanded his followers to love one another as he had loved them. In sending Jesus, God was doing something new in the world.

"Light" is a symbol of truth, goodness, and love. You cannot claim to be walking in the light if you hate your brother or sister. "Brother" and "sister" in 1 John 2:11 probably refer to fellow Christians. The New Testament focuses on the importance of unity and fellowship within the church. In times of persecution, Christians had to lean on one another. Of course, Jesus also commanded us to love our neighbors as ourselves, and so we can easily expand this instruction to love as reaching beyond the church also. If we love fellow Christians, "there is no cause for stumbling." Love causes us to walk uprightly and will also keep us from tripping others.

Hatred brings opposite results. To hate another believer means you are not yourself in the family of believers, but you are walking in darkness. That darkness makes you lose your way, and you will be floundering to find it. In fact, the darkness blinds you so you cannot see. A good question to ask yourself is, *Do I really see the people around me, or do I perceive only an annoying crowd?*

A Possible Poetic Interlude (2:12–17)

John broke his line of thought here to address his readers directly. He wrote a sort of *round-robin*, cycling through three kinds of readers twice in 1 John 2:13–14. He addressed "little children," "fathers," and "young people." The words "little children" may have referred to newer Christians, who had only recently found forgiveness and come to know God. By "fathers," he may have addressed the elders in the community. Elders had authority and respect in Jewish life, and that authority likely carried over into churches. "Young people" likely included the rest of the church. Those we think of as teenagers today were adults in that society, serving as apprentices and raising families. The strength of young adulthood is implied in the words "conquered" (2:13) and "strong" (2:14). Where would you place yourself in this list? Note especially that John saw the church as a family, a good family, a loving family. In that family each person, each group, had its part to play.

The next three verses (2:15–17) can be thought of as part of this greeting or a separate section. In either case, John combined the themes of love and obedience. John instructed, "Do not love the world or the things in the world" (2:15). In other places (see John 3:16), "world" means people in general. Here, however, "world" points to temporary and sinful culture rather than to God's way and to darkness, not light.

Some have pointed out the same three attitudes mentioned in 1 John 2:16 led Eve to sin in Genesis 3:6. John may well have had that verse in mind here. Eve first saw the fruit looked "good for food" ("the desire of the flesh"); it was "a delight to the eyes" ("desire of the eyes"), and that she would become "wise" ("pride"). The New Revised Standard Version reads "pride in riches," but the New American Standard Bible has "pride of life," which is a more direct translation of the Greek.

John saw a tension in our relationship with the world. We too are tempted by things that look good, might feel good, and even might seem to benefit us for a while. Yet these are temporary pleasures that eventually lead to destruction. We are to follow light, not darkness.

Belief in the Last Hour (2:18–27)

"The last hour"—The Old Testament speaks of a coming day of judgment. In Amos 5:18–20, the prophet denounced those who thought they wanted to see "the Day of the LORD." They were looking for the Lord to come and defeat their enemies. Amos told them the day would be one of "darkness, not light," because of their sin (Amos 5:18). Does that remind you of 1 John?

The church was aware of the coming of "the antichrist." John agreed that "the antichrist" not only would come but had already come. Indeed, "many antichrists" had come. The word "antichrist" simply means *one who is against Christ.* Through use, the term grew to mean an archvillain, the devil incarnate. But rather than one super-villain, John saw a broader picture—numerous traitors. Their appearance was a sign that "the last hour" had come. John might have been writing a particular

HOW CAN I PUT THESE TEACHINGS INTO PRACTICE?

- Choose a teaching of Christ you have trouble obeying. For one day, seek to follow that truth.

- Choose a church member whom you find it difficult to deal with. Don't seek him or her out, but remember the next time you face each other to treat that person as you would want him or her to treat you.

- Can you state clearly in words your belief about Jesus? Perhaps you could write a paragraph expressing that belief. Another possibility would be to discuss those beliefs with another class member.

church that had seen many members leave. Or several groups might have been pulling away from the church over disputed teaching.

These "antichrists" apparently had been associated with the churches in some way and then had deserted them. John insisted that their leaving proved they were never a genuine part. True Christians remain a vital part of the body of Christ.

In verse 20, John said, his readers had been "anointed by the Holy One, and all of you have knowledge." The anointing probably points to the Holy Spirit, given to each Christian. There were groups of Christians with a Greek background who were accustomed to speaking of secret knowledge (see the small article, "Knowledge"). Many in these groups believed Jesus was indeed God but only appeared to be human and only appeared to die. John emphasized that Christians did not need a secret knowledge. The Spirit had given them real knowledge.

Verse 21 indicates that John knew he was *preaching to the choir*, as we sometimes say. They already knew what he was writing, and they also knew that lies and truth don't fit together. The liar denied that "Jesus is the Christ," the Messiah, the Anointed One. And if they didn't understand Christ, they didn't understand the Father. Both here and in the Gospel of John, God and Christ are inseparable. John defined "the antichrist" as "the one who denies the Father and the Son" (2:22). You can't deny Jesus and have the Father. But to confess Christ is also to confess the true God.

John believed his readers began the Christian life correctly. He urged them to remain true to the first teachings. If they did, their lives would be united with God through Christ. They, in turn, would remain faithful and receive the promised reward of eternal life.

John wrote to warn them of the liars and deceivers they would meet (2:26). Yet he was sure that "the anointing" they received from the Spirit would guide them into truth (2:27). This "anointing" produced many benefits. It remained with them, never leaving, and the same anointing guided them to right understanding, even without a teacher. The anointing taught them all things. There was no secret knowledge that others had to teach them or that they had to acquire. The Spirit of Christ would stay with them and never deceive them. Thus, they should remain fixed on Christ.

Applying the Lesson to Life

Obedience, love, and belief in Christ are three values emphasized in this portion of Scripture. To be an effective Christian, we need all three. Obedience means following the teachings of Scripture, especially those of Christ. Love means to develop a warm, outgoing, helpful relationship with others that originates in your close relationship to God. Finally, you must have Christ in the right place in your mind and heart. He is the Son of the Living God, who died for our sins and was raised to share his life with us!

QUESTIONS

1. John said that truth is something you do (2:4). Based on your actions, how obedient are you to Christ?

2. Part of obedience is love for one another, and love makes obedience easier. How rich is your love for God and for fellow church members?

3. Are you a prisoner of your culture? Are you constantly flirting with temptation? What can you do to separate yourself from cultural values that lead people astray?

4. What to you is the importance of knowing Jesus as the divine Son of God, whose death on the cross brought us salvation? Is this belief central to your faith?

MAIN IDEA
We can prepare confidently
for the future by living as
God's children today.

QUESTION TO EXPLORE
How can we face our
future with confidence?

STUDY AIM
To identify ways for facing
my future with confidence

QUICK READ
By pursuing an intimate
relationship with Christ and
refusing to tolerate sin in
our lives, we live as God's
children today and can face
the future with confidence.

LESSON NINE
Facing the Future with Confidence

I met Ruth[1] while working at a temp agency one summer. A committed Christian, Ruth told me that before she accepted Christ she had been very interested in knowing the future. She spent time and money on anything she thought would help her know the future, including horoscopes, tarot cards, and psychic hotlines. Ruth said she was first introduced to Christ by a friend who noticed her interest in the future. Ruth's friend told her that if she really wanted to know the future, she needed to know the One who controls the future.

Ruth's friend gave her a New Testament, which Ruth read out of curiosity. Through the Bible, Ruth came to understand that only God knows the future and that a relationship with Jesus Christ is the only way we can face the future with confidence.

Ruth was not alone in her desire to know the future. A quick glance at the headlines or the evening news shows many people making predictions about what's going to happen in the future. Why are we so interested in the future? Perhaps it is the sense that knowing what is coming gives us control.

As Ruth discovered, however, God is the only one who knows what the future will hold. We do not even know what tomorrow will bring. Still, there are some things we do know. God's reign is sure. Jesus will return. There will be a day when God will exercise judgment over humanity. As Christians, we can face that day with confidence when we live as God's children today.[2]

1 JOHN 2:28–29

[28] Now, little children, abide in Him, so that when He appears, we may have confidence and not shrink away from Him in shame at His coming. [29] If you know that He is righteous, you know that everyone also who practices righteousness is born of Him.

1 JOHN 3:1–10

[1] See how great a love the Father has bestowed on us, that we would be called children of God; and such we are. For this reason the world does not know us, because it did not know Him.

² Beloved, now we are children of God, and it has not appeared as yet what we will be. We know that when He appears, we will be like Him, because we will see Him just as He is. ³ And everyone who has this hope fixed on Him purifies himself, just as He is pure. ⁴ Everyone who practices sin also practices lawlessness; and sin is lawlessness. ⁵ You know that He appeared in order to take away sins; and in Him there is no sin. ⁶ No one who abides in Him sins; no one who sins has seen Him or knows Him. ⁷ Little children, make sure no one deceives you; the one who practices righteousness is righteous, just as He is righteous; ⁸ the one who practices sin is of the devil; for the devil has sinned from the beginning. The Son of God appeared for this purpose, to destroy the works of the devil. ⁹ No one who is born of God practices sin, because His seed abides in him; and he cannot sin, because he is born of God. ¹⁰ By this the children of God and the children of the devil are obvious: anyone who does not practice righteousness is not of God, nor the one who does not love his brother.

Confident Through Abiding (2:28–29)

One of the greatest moments in my day is when my children and I hear the garage door open as my husband comes home. It doesn't matter what the kids are involved in. As soon as they hear him coming in, they drop what they're doing and run to him. They greet him with joy and confidence, sure of their welcome.

In verse 28, John urges us to "abide in Him," so that when Jesus comes "we may have confidence and not shrink away from Him in shame." Living now in the presence of Christ means we don't have to be ashamed at his coming. Often we think of eternal life as something that begins after death, but by pursing a relationship with God today, we can experience eternal life now. Jesus defined eternal life this way: "This is eternal life, that they may know You, the only true God, and Jesus Christ whom You have sent" (John 17:3). *Abiding in Christ* is the practice of eternal life in the present; it is knowing God and experiencing God's love as we walk in daily dependence on Christ. Our relationship with God *now* prepares us for Jesus' coming.

As we abide in Christ, we come to reflect God's character. Since we know that God is righteous, we also know that "everyone . . . who practices righteousness" belongs to God. John defined doing righteousness as more than just *playing nice*. Rather, righteousness is obediently confessing Jesus Christ as Lord and demonstrating love to one's brothers and sisters in Christ. We practice righteousness when we practice genuine faith and loving obedience to God's commands. Righteousness is a sign of being "born of Him" (2:29). Both the Gospel of John and 1 John use the image of a second birth to describe the experience of coming to saving faith in Christ. When we commit our lives to Christ, we experience such a radical transformation that it is as if we have begun a new life, or been "born again" (John 3:3).

Confident in His Love (3:1–3)

God proves the greatness of his love by calling us his "children." His love is not something we earn or deserve; it is a gift God has "bestowed" (NASB) or "lavished" (NIV) on us (1 John 3:1). As God's children, we should not be surprised when the unbelieving world rejects us; in fact, such rejection is proof of our status. The world did not know Christ either (John 1:10).

My husband strongly resembles his father. When we go home, it's common to hear people say, *Well, you can't deny him!* because they look so much alike. Similarly, as children of God we should reflect God's likeness. The Christian life is a process of growing to look more like Christ. In our attitudes, our actions, and our responses to other people and situations, we are transformed so what we do is more like what Jesus would do. Instead of seeking vengeance, we forgive. Instead of shunning others, we embrace them. Instead of hoarding money, possessions, or time, we give generously. Instead of seeking our own benefit in relationships, we consider others' needs. This transformation is an outworking of the Holy Spirit in our lives, as the Spirit teaches, corrects, and refines us. However, the process is not automatic. We must commit ourselves to the change.

Many people today like to talk about being "children of God" (1 John 3:1). Some say that since we are all God's creation, we are all God's children. This line of thinking is common among a growing number of people. One common feature of this claim that *we are all God's children* is the lack of expectations. Many people seem to want the status of being God's children without the commitment it implies.

This is not what John means by being "children of God." We, who have experienced God's love through Jesus Christ, been forgiven of our sins, and adopted as sons and daughters of God, have received an enormous privilege. Yet, with that privilege comes responsibility. The great hope of the Christian life is that we will one day see God face to face (3:2). It is not something that we merely wish for; hope is the sure expectation that God will keep his promises. Our certain hope does not excuse us from the responsibility of preparing for Christ's coming. Those who hope to see God must purify themselves because God himself is pure (3:3).

Confident in His Righteousness (3:4–10)

John continued to define who God's children are meant to be by showing what we are *not* meant to be. We are *not* meant to be people characterized by sin and disobedience to God. John's argument is simple. Everyone

OPPOSING THEMES IN 1 JOHN

One of the dominant features of 1 John is the use of opposing themes: love and hate; light and dark; church and world; Jesus and antichrist; children of God and children of the devil. It is not that John sees two equal and opposing forces at work, but that he sees only two alternatives. Either we belong to God and God's kingdom, or we fall under Satan's influence over the unredeemed world.

This thought can be difficult for modern readers to accept. Even Christians sometimes see the world in shades of gray. When it comes to salvation, however, there is no middle way. Either we confess Jesus as Lord and Savior or we do not. Our lives give evidence that we belong to God, or they prove that we do not know him.

The opposing themes in 1 John remind us we have only two options for our eternal home: heaven or hell. Thankfully, 1 John also tells us how we can have confidence we are truly God's children— genuine faith in Christ proved by righteousness and genuine love.

who sins breaks God's law. By God's law, John does not mean the Old Testament law as much as it means simply what God has willed or commanded. Sin, or lawlessness, is rebellion against God's authority. Christ came to take away our sins, and Christ himself never sinned. It would be impossible for one who had sinned to take away sins. Both the children of God and the children of the devil are known by their fruits—either righteousness or sin. Jesus came to defeat the devil and destroy his works. No one who knows Christ continues to sin because God's seed cannot produce continuing sin. When people do not practice righteousness and do not love others, they prove they do not belong to God (3:10).

The arguments are simple, but the implications are complex. What does it mean that "no one who is born of God practices sin?" (3:9). Earlier in the letter, John acknowledged that Christians still sin (1:8). How can we reconcile the two statements?

One possible explanation is that in the original language the phrase "practices sin" indicates an ongoing state or lifestyle of rebellion against God, something that is difficult to express in an English translation. Another possibility is that John was reacting against a heretical group, the Gnostics, that emphasized the spiritual over the physical. Some Gnostics taught that what happens in our physical bodies does not affect our spiritual nature. They used this separation between the physical and the spiritual to excuse immoral behavior. Either way, John made it clear that ongoing sinful behavior should not characterize the life of a Christian. He said that God's "seed" cannot produce sin. Some think God's "seed" may be a reference to Christians as descendants or children of God. Others think it may be a reference to the indwelling of the Holy Spirit. We can say with certainty that God's holiness does not lead to sinful disobedience.

CASE STUDY:

You have had a visitor attend your Bible study group over the last several weeks. The visitor seems to have some interest in Christianity but doesn't demonstrate a clear understanding of the gospel. One day during your lesson the visitor comments that *we are all God's children* and questions how a loving God could send anyone to hell. How could you respond?

The reality is that because of our human nature we still sin. John made it clear that when we do sin, God forgives us when we confess it (1 John 1:9). Still, much like the Gnostics of John's time, sometimes we use our human nature as an excuse for sin. We may toss around phrases like *Christians aren't perfect, just forgiven.* God's grace, though, is a cause for praise and thanksgiving, not something to be taken for granted. These verses are meant to challenge us, and we should not fall into the trap of explaining them away so we can go on with life as usual. Yes, John does seem to be talking about a life characterized by ongoing sin. But most of our sins probably are habitual. When God convicts of sin, the proper response is not to make excuses. The proper response to sin is confession and repentance. Sin is not something we should tolerate; it is something we should seek to overcome.

In verse 10, John summarized two of the tests of faith he discussed in 1 John 2:18–27: righteousness and Christian love. Here, John said that these tests are a way we can identify those who truly belong to God. John gives only two options—either we are "children of God" or we are "children of the devil." The devil, or Satan, is the leader of all spiritual forces in rebellion against God. Although defeated at the cross, the devil still has power to tempt and exercises his authority over the unredeemed world (Ephesians 2:2; 6:12; John 12:31;1 John 5:19). Those who do not belong to God are under Satan's influence and authority and are therefore "children of the devil."

Our actions demonstrate where our allegiance lies. Those who practice righteousness and love their fellow Christians prove they are children of God.

Implications and Actions

We are privileged to know the end of the story. One day, Jesus will return in victory and put an end to sin and death. That day will be a day of great celebration, but it will also be a day of great judgment. We can have confidence at Jesus' coming by living in his presence today. Our hope of seeing God face to face should motivate us to prepare for that day.

As we do what is right, purify ourselves from sin, and love our fellow believers, we can have confidence that we belong to God. Those who are God's children will stand before him unashamed.

QUESTIONS

1. How should our belief in Jesus' future coming affect how we live our lives today?

2. What are some of the privileges and responsibilities that come with being known as children of God?

3. How would you explain the difference between the idea that *we are all God's children* and a biblical understanding of being a child of God?

4. How does knowing your status as a child of God give you confidence about the future?

5. Is there an area of your life where you have tolerated sin and need to repent?

NOTES

1. Name has been changed.

2. Unless otherwise indicated, all Scripture quotations in lessons 9–11 are from the New American Standard Bible (1995 edition).

Loving to the Nth Degree

FOCAL TEXT
1 John 3:11–18; 4:7–12, 19–21

BACKGROUND
1 John 3:11—4:21

MAIN IDEA
Loving one another in our acts and not just in our words is an essential part of being Christian.

QUESTION TO EXPLORE
Why does Scripture insist on the importance of genuine love?

STUDY AIM
To evaluate the extent to which genuine love characterizes my life and identify ways in which I will increase my responsiveness to God's love

QUICK READ
Loving one another in our actions and not just our words is an essential part of being Christian and a proof of genuine faith.

When my husband was called as pastor to our first church, the former pastor told us it was the most loving congregation he had ever served. During the almost five years we spent in this rural congregation, we found his words to be true.

Members of the congregation took care of one another. Whether it was rides to and from chemotherapy treatments, prayer for one another, or helping provide a young widow with funeral expenses, the church met one another's needs. They also extended that love to the community. When a utility worker was killed in a tragic accident, two of our church members were the first on hand with food and supplies for the recovery crew. When a family lost everything to a house fire, the church rallied to provide for their needs.

Our family also experienced the benefits of their loving care. When the tires on both our cars were slashed, the church replaced them for us. They blessed us abundantly when both our children were born and helped us remodel our home.

It wasn't a perfect church by any means, but they loved us and they loved one another. Our experience there gave us a picture of church as it is meant to be—God's love demonstrated in our love for one another.

1 JOHN 3:11–18

11 For this is the message which you have heard from the beginning, that we should love one another; 12 not as Cain, who was of the evil one and slew his brother. And for what reason did he slay him? Because his deeds were evil, and his brother's were righteous. 13 Do not be surprised, brethren, if the world hates you. 14 We know that we have passed out of death into life, because we love the brethren. He who does not love abides in death. 15 Everyone who hates his brother is a murderer; and you know that no murderer has eternal life abiding in him. 16 We know love by this, that He laid down His life for us; and we ought to lay down our lives for the brethren. 17 But whoever has the world's goods, and sees his brother in need and closes his heart against him, how does the love of God abide in him? 18 Little children, let us not love with word or with tongue, but in deed and truth.

1 JOHN 4:7–12, 19–21

[7] Beloved, let us love one another, for love is from God; and everyone who loves is born of God and knows God. [8] The one who does not love does not know God, for God is love. [9] By this the love of God was manifested in us, that God has sent His only begotten Son into the world so that we might live through Him. [10] In this is love, not that we loved God, but that He loved us and sent His Son to be the propitiation for our sins. [11] Beloved, if God so loved us, we also ought to love one another. [12] No one has seen God at any time; if we love one another, God abides in us, and His love is perfected in us.

. . . .

[19] We love, because He first loved us. [20] If someone says, "I love God," and hates his brother, he is a liar; for the one who does not love his brother whom he has seen, cannot love God whom he has not seen. [21] And this commandment we have from Him, that the one who loves God should love his brother also.

Love Not Hate (3:11–18)

As we saw in the previous lesson, John was discussing the tests of genuine faith. Beginning in verse 11, John focused on one test in particular: the test of genuine love. John reminded his readers that from their first hearing of the gospel they had heard that Christians should love one another (1 John 3:11). John's letter echoes the words of Christ: "A new commandment I give to you, that you love one another, even as I have loved you, that you also love one another" (John 13:34).

John began his explanation of what genuine love looks like by first giving an example of what love does *not* look like: Cain, who committed the first murder recorded in Scripture. Genesis 4 tells the story. Adam and Eve had two sons, Cain and Abel. Abel was a shepherd, but Cain was a farmer. Both men brought sacrifices to God; Abel brought a lamb from his flock, but Cain brought some of his produce. God accepted Abel's offering but rejected Cain's, apparently because Cain's motives in offering his sacrifice were not right. Motivated by his jealousy and rage, Cain killed Abel and was judged by God.

John gave an additional reason for Cain's murder of his brother: "because his deeds were evil, and his brother's were righteous" (1 John 3:12). John went on to say that as Christians, we should not be surprised if the world hates us (3:13). The tense of the verb used for *hate* in verse 13 does not indicate an occasional occurrence, but a present, abiding state. Like Cain, those who have rejected God and God's word often react with envy and hatred against the church because the righteous deeds of God's people reveal the true nature of their wickedness.

In contrast to the world's hate, Christians are marked by genuine love. John said that believers can have confidence we have "passed out of death into life" if we love one another (3:14). Love for our fellow believers is one sign of our salvation and a criterion by which we can test our membership in the kingdom of God.

If love is a sign of membership in the kingdom, lack of love is a sign of exclusion from it. John's equation of hatred and murder in verse 15 may seem strong, but hatred is a strong word. To hate someone is to wish that the other person does not exist, to refuse to recognize his or her personal worth, and even to long for that person to be dead. John echoed the words of Christ in the Sermon on the Mount (Matthew 5:21–22). As anyone who lusts has committed adultery in his or her heart (Matt. 5:27–28), one who hates has committed murder in the heart. Murder— like most sins—begins not with the action but with an attitude that is allowed to grow in the mind and heart until it comes to fruition.

If Cain demonstrated the opposite of love, Jesus defines it. Jesus is both the source of love and the example we should emulate. Christ demonstrated his love by laying down his life for us. In the same way, we should be willing to sacrifice for our brothers and sisters in Christ. As Jesus laid down his life, we should also be willing to lay down our lives.

Most of us will never be called on to literally sacrifice our lives to save someone else. John made it clear he was talking about not only a potential moment of great sacrifice, but also a lifestyle of service and humility to others. We are not called to sacrifice only in moments of great crisis, but also to meet the needs of our fellow believers on an ongoing basis. Christ's sacrifice should motivate us to sacrifice for others. Love must be more than an emotion; love is real only when demonstrated in action.

John's focus in this passage is on love for our fellow Christians. We know God loved the world enough that Jesus died for it. God's heart for the lost is evident throughout Scripture. It is only natural as we grow in our love for God and for one another that we will also grow in our love for the world. Why then did John have such a seemingly narrow focus here?

One reason for John's focus on love among believers might be that he was writing to a church who had experienced conflict. False teachers had arisen in the church and then left the fellowship (1 John 2:18–20). The remaining church members needed to be reminded how Christians should treat one another. A second reason might be that if we as Christians do not love one another and meet one another's needs, we will never be able to love the world. If we cannot love those who have joined with us in following Christ and are indwelt by the Holy Spirit, how can we love those who are lost and act out of their sinful nature?

WILLIAM KNIBB: EMANCIPATION IN JAMAICA

William Knibb (1803–1845) was twenty-one years old when he went to Jamaica to continue the missionary work of his brother, Tom, who had died after only three months of service.

On arriving in Jamaica, Knibb soon realized that for the gospel to spread in Jamaica, slavery must be eradicated. The slave owners, many of whom had professed Christianity, were outraged at Knibb's work and opposed him. Some swore they would kill their slaves before granting them freedom. The slave owners finally succeeded in having Knibb imprisoned.

After his release, Knibb returned to England to urge English Baptists to stand against slavery. He met with initial opposition, but Knibb's conviction and love for the people of Jamaica were too great to be silenced. For two years he traveled through England and Scotland, preaching fervently against the slave trade.

Knibb won the battle. The British Parliament declared that all colonial slaves would be set free at midnight on July 31, 1833. Knibb hurried back to Jamaica and was there to celebrate the emancipation of the people he loved. [1]

Sometimes the people who are closest to us are the hardest to love. This is true in churches but also in families. Sometimes we overlook our immediate family's needs because we do not see them. We can easily see the family having trouble making ends meet because of job loss. It can be more difficult to see the needs of our spouses and children because they are intangible—for quality time, a listening ear, a healthy touch. We dare not become so busy meeting the needs of those around us that we forget our family's most important need: our attentive presence.

Verses 19–22 are not in our focal passage, but perhaps a comment about them would be helpful. In these verses, John said love gives us confidence before God. The original language leaves room for a variety of interpretations of these difficult verses. John said we "will know" we are "of the truth." This could be a reference to God's final judgment, or John could be thinking of some occasion when we question our salvation. Either way, John said that our love and obedience can give us confidence before God.

God Is Love (4:7–12)

In 1 John 4:1–6, John dealt with the theme of right belief before returning to the idea of Christian love in verse 7. We will study verses 1–6 in

---

WAYS TO APPLY THIS LESSON:

- Is there anyone in your church family with whom you have a broken relationship? How could you demonstrate love to that person?

- With your Bible study group, think of one way you could show love by practically meeting the needs of someone in your church family. Consider families experiencing economic stress, students working their way through school, military families on deployment, and shut-ins who need home repairs done.

- To whom could you show love by the gift of your presence? Plan to spend time with that person.

detail in lesson eleven. In verse 7, John again exhorts us as believers to love one another, but focuses here on the reason: love comes from God.

Verse 8 contains one of John's great declarations about the nature of God: God is love. God by his very nature is love; all God's actions are loving. God is loving in his mercy, and God is loving in his justice. We who know God must reflect God's character.

It is important to note that "God is love," not that *love is God.* In our culture, we often make *love* an idol and use *being in love* to excuse all kinds of actions, even breaking our wedding vows because we have now *fallen in love* with someone else. If God is love, his character must define what love is.

This definition of love is precisely what John offered in verses 9–10. Echoing Jesus' words in John 3:16, John said in verse 9 that God demonstrates his love by sending Christ into the world "that we might live through Him." This act of love says more about God than it does about us. One characteristic of God's love is its unconditional nature. Some first-century Jewish writers attempted to portray God's love as the result of our own worth, but John refuted this. The important thing is not that we loved God, but that God loved us. God loved us first and sent his Son as the payment or atoning sacrifice for our sins.

Verse 11 is John's conclusion: "If God so loved us, we also ought to love one another." We cannot see God, but when we love one another we experience God's presence. The unseen God, revealed in Christ, now resides in his people in the presence of the Holy Spirit. By the power of the Spirit, God's love is demonstrated in our relationships with one another.

Because God First Loved Us (4:19–21)

In this summary section, John returned to his main point: we love because God first loved us (4:19). John reiterated the incompatibility between loving God and hating one another. He explained one way in which our love for one another can be a proof of our love for God. Since God is unseen, it might be possible for someone to go through the motions of faith and deceive others into believing he or she loves God. It is much harder to fake love for a person we can see. If we cannot love those we can see, feel, and touch, how can we love the invisible God? If we love God, we must also love one another.

Implications and Actions

The historical context of 1 John makes John's emphasis on love seem even more amazing. In addition to the conflict with the group that had left the church over their false doctrine, the church was experiencing persecution, and members were themselves objects of hate. Yet John never advocated hate in return—only love. His audience had every excuse to fear and to hate, but John wrote that the love of God has the power to cast out both. Love is the great characteristic of God's people and evidence of genuine faith.

Like John's original audience, sometimes we face challenging circumstances for love. Christians, even strong Christians, are not perfect. Sometimes we make mistakes. Sometimes we hurt one another. Sometimes we just plain *don't like* one another. But we are called to love one another anyway. God loved us when we were unlovable. He gives us the power to love as he loved—forgiving, meeting physical needs, giving the gift of our presence.

Platitudes are easy. The kind of genuine love that requires us to give something of ourselves is much harder. Yet when we get it right, the world takes notice. Only God's power explains genuine love.

QUESTIONS

1. How does genuine love demonstrate genuine faith?

2. How has God demonstrated his love to you through the actions of fellow Christians?

3. What is the difference in saying that "God is love" and that *love is God*? How does a correct understanding of God's love affect our actions?

4. Why do you think loving our fellow believers is so important?
   What are the consequences of a failure to love?

5. How can you show your love in a concrete way to someone this
   week?

NOTES

1. Benjamin P. Browne, *Tales of Baptist Daring* (Philadelphia, Judson Press: 1961), 97–105.
   See also www.bmsworldmission.org/standard.aspx?id=8791. Accessed 4/22/10.

FOCAL TEXT
1 John 4:1–6, 13–16a

BACKGROUND
1 John 4:1–6, 13–16a

MAIN IDEA
Belief in Jesus as God's
Son who really became
human is an essential for
authentic Christianity.

QUESTION TO EXPLORE
How important is right
belief in the Christian life?

STUDY AIM
To affirm or re-affirm my
belief in Jesus as God's
divine-human Son

QUICK READ
Believing in Jesus as God's
divine-human Son gives
confidence before God
and helps to identify true
followers of Christ.

LESSON ELEVEN
Believing in God's Divine-Human Son

My husband and I spent our early ministry together in international student outreach through Baptist Student Ministries at the University of Washington. One of the challenges we faced was helping new believers and seekers distinguish between campus groups that taught genuine Christianity and those that did not.

We were pleased to work with many Christian groups on campus, but there were also those that professed to follow Christ but taught very different doctrines. Several had their own versions of the Bible. One group taught that Jesus was a *mingling* of God and man and we could follow in his example by *mingling* with God and becoming part of God's nature. For our international students, many of whom had little grounding in Christian teaching, it was sometimes difficult to understand the distinctions or why the distinctions were important.

In his letters John was writing to a group of Christians who needed to correctly understand who Jesus was. This group of believers had been influenced by false teachers who denied Jesus' humanity. One of John's goals in writing was to remind them of the importance of believing in both Jesus' humanity and his divinity.

1 JOHN 4:1–6, 13–16A

[1] Beloved, do not believe every spirit, but test the spirits to see whether they are from God, because many false prophets have gone out into the world. [2] By this you know the Spirit of God: every spirit that confesses that Jesus Christ has come in the flesh is from God; [3] and every spirit that does not confess Jesus is not from God; this is the spirit of the antichrist, of which you have heard that it is coming, and now it is already in the world. [4] You are from God, little children, and have overcome them; because greater is He who is in you than he who is in the world. [5] They are from the world; therefore they speak as from the world, and the world listens to them. [6] We are from God; he who knows God listens to us; he who is not from God does not listen to us. By this we know the spirit of truth and the spirit of error.

· ·

¹³ By this we know that we abide in Him and He in us, because He has given us of His Spirit. ¹⁴ We have seen and testify that the Father has sent the Son to be the Savior of the world. ¹⁵ Whoever confesses that Jesus is the Son of God, God abides in him, and he in God. ¹⁶ We have come to know and have believed the love which God has for us.

Test the Spirits (4:1–3)

The Roman Empire was a world full of spiritual activity. In addition to genuine Christianity, John's readers would have been acquainted with Greco-Roman religions with their own sets of temples, prophets, and oracles. There were also the so-called *mystery* religions such as Mithraism. These mystery religions revealed their secrets only to their followers but also had practices such as baptism that at times resembled Christianity. The New Testament also gives evidence of false teachers who rose up in various times and places and distorted the basic teaching of the gospel while still claiming the name of Christ.

It is in this environment that John urged his readers to "test the spirits . . . because many false prophets have gone out into the world" (1 John 4:1). It can be tempting to credit any charismatic speaker or unusual spiritual occurrence as being inspired by God, but in both John's time and ours spiritual forces are at work that are not from God. Satan, the great deceiver, is always at work doing what he can to distract people from true allegiance to Christ. We need to test whether those who claim to speak for God really belong to him.

John gave one simple test: those who affirm both Jesus' deity and his humanity belong to God (4:3). The most important test for genuine belief is what a person or a group claims about Jesus. If their teachings do not agree with the portrait of Jesus as presented in Scripture, we must reject their teaching.

In this passage, John focused on one particular false teaching. The false teachers John combated in this letter belonged to a group that denied Jesus' humanity. As one of Jesus' closest followers, John was uniquely qualified to affirm Jesus' humanity. John himself had seen Jesus with his eyes and had touched him with his hands. He thus was able to testify to both Jesus' humanity and deity (1:1–4). The false teachers, however, denied Jesus' humanity. They may have been an early part of the Gnostic movement, a group that tended to emphasize the spiritual world and see the physical world as evil (see small article, "Gnostics").

In contrast, John insisted that both Jesus' divinity and his humanity are essential parts of the gospel message. If Jesus was not both fully divine and fully human, the entire message of salvation falls apart. If Jesus was only somehow pretending to be human, we lose the conviction and confidence of being able to follow Jesus' example of a life fully obedient to God. It is only in Jesus' humanity that he is able to identify with and yet triumph over our temptations (Hebrews 4:15). Yet if Jesus was not truly God, how could his death bring us salvation? It is impossible for the death of a mere human being to pay for any single person's sins, much less the sins of the entire world. If Jesus was only a moral man and a good teacher, he would have been a martyr but not the Savior. His death had to be real in order to be sacrificial. If Jesus had only seemed to die or pretended to die, could we really say he had sacrificed himself for us? Could a pretense of death inspire us to sacrifice for and love our brothers and sisters in Christ? Jesus' death is proof of his humanity. Only a human being could truly die. Only God could redeem us from sin and reconcile us to himself. True belief in Christ means belief in both Jesus' divinity and his humanity.

John said that any spirit "that does not confess Jesus is . . . the spirit of the antichrist" (1 John 4:3). Here John used "antichrist" to describe one who is against Christ, or who while pretending to look like Jesus works to oppose Jesus and his mission. While earlier in his letter John wrote of the "antichrist" who is to come at the end of time (2:18), here he used the term to describe those already at work in the world in opposition to Christ. There will come a day when Satan will make his final stand, but he still exercises his influence today in those who distort the gospel message and deny Jesus' identity as fully God and fully man.

Greater Is He Who Is in You (4:4–6)

John reminded the church that they had already overcome the false teachers by refusing to accept their distortion of the gospel. The church's victory was not because of their own strength, but because the Spirit of Christ alive in them is greater than "he who is in the world," Satan.

John also gave a second test for identifying false teachers. Who are they influencing? John said that because the false teachers were "of the world," the world listened to them (1 John 4:5). In 2 Timothy, Paul spoke of a time when people will reject sound doctrine in favor of those who *tickle their ears* and tell them what they want to hear (2 Timothy 4:3). When a new teacher begins attracting a following, one thing to consider is the audience he or she attracts. Are their followers mature believers who are firmly grounded in the word of God, or are they new converts and seekers whose faith has not yet been tested? Unlike the false teachers, those who know God respect the teachings and counsel of the Christian community.

By This We Know (4:13–16a)

In chapter 3, John said that genuine Christian love is a sign of true Christianity. In this passage, John gave two additional tests: true

---

GNOSTICS

One of the greatest challenges to early Christianity was the Gnostic movement. While Gnosticism was mainly a second-century phenomenon, many scholars believe that the false teachers John combated in his letters represented an early form of the Gnostic movement.

Gnosticism gets its name from the Greek word *gnosis*, meaning *knowledge*. Gnostics believed the key to salvation lay in secret knowledge revealed only to a few. Gnostics believed all matter was evil, including the body. According to the Gnostics, human beings were spirits imprisoned in a human body. The goal was to escape from the body and the physical world. Some Gnostics believed Christ was a heavenly messenger sent to give the secret knowledge needed to escape the physical world. Since they believed matter was evil, the Gnostics denied Christ's humanity. Some said Jesus did not have a body like ours; others distinguished between *Jesus* and *Christ* by claiming the spirit of Christ descended on Jesus at his baptism but left before his death.

CASE STUDY

One of your co-workers is a young woman who attends the local community college. She has been attending a Bible study hosted by a group on campus and has been enthusiastic about the friends she is making. One day she confides in you that while the group seems friendly, she is beginning to feel uncomfortable with some of their teachings. What advice would you give?

Christians have the Holy Spirit and have confessed Jesus as the Son of God. False prophets and teachers may well be inspired—but not by the Spirit of God.

One sign of true Christianity is the presence of the Holy Spirit. Those who have repented of their sins and committed to follow Jesus as Lord have received the gift of the Holy Spirit. In receiving the Spirit we do not become God, but we receive the gift of God's indwelling presence. Christianity is first and foremost a relationship with God. We know we have received the Spirit when we experience the benefits of that relationship. When we have confidence in prayer, when God speaks to us through his word, when we experience God working in us through our spiritual gifts, then we know we have the Holy Spirit within us. The presence of the Holy Spirit in our lives assures us of our salvation.

The second test is that of right belief. True Christians confess that God sent Jesus "to be the Savior of the world" (1 John 4:14). One of the things that make Christianity unique is that it is rooted in history. Some antagonists of Christianity may claim that many of the ancient religions tell the story of a dying and rising god or some sort of blend between the divine and the human. But Christianity embraces a God who willingly laid aside the privileges of deity to take on all humanity's frailty. In so doing, God took the price of our redemption on himself. Jesus did not make his sacrifice in the realm of legend and myth; rather he stepped into history at a specific place and specific point in time. The penalty of death we pay for our sins is real; no mere legend would be enough to pay it. True Christian doctrine must include a belief in the historic reality of Jesus' incarnation, death, burial, and resurrection.

John, however, did not say only that we must *believe* that Jesus is the Son of God; he said that we must *confess* it (4:15). What does it mean to *confess*? To *confess* something is not just acknowledging a historical fact; *confessing* is an expression of obedient trust. It is both a public acknowledgment and an expression of commitment. To call him Jesus is recognition of his humanity. The title *Son of God* is a declaration of his divinity. Confessing that Jesus is the Son of God means acknowledging both. It is an expression of faith in God's divine-human Son. God took the initiative in his relationship with us by sending Jesus. When we respond with obedient trust, we live in God, and God lives in us.

Only through Jesus can we understand the depth of God's love for us. God's love for us is revealed in Jesus' incarnation, death, and resurrection. Without confessing Jesus as the Son of God, we cannot know God's love. When we make the commitment of faith to Jesus as Savior, fully human and fully divine, we intimately experience God's love for us (4:16).

Implications and Actions

One thing this passage gives me is *confidence*. I know I have confessed my faith in Jesus as Son of God and Savior and experience the work of the Holy Spirit in my life. This reality gives me confidence that I belong to God. Perhaps, though, as you have studied this lesson you do not have that same confidence. It may be that at one point you followed Jesus as Lord but have allowed sin to creep back into your life and no longer feel you hear from God. Or, it may be that you have never repented of your sins and confessed Jesus as Lord. If God is convicting your heart today, don't wait. Humble yourself before God, repent, seek God's face, and act in obedience to whatever God tells you to do.

Another thing this passage gives me is *caution*. Many charismatic, spiritual speakers are at work today. We must exercise discernment in the teachings we accept. Anyone who claims to possess spiritual truth but does not confess Jesus Christ does not speak for God. God has given us his word and his Spirit so we can discern the truth. By investing ourselves in truth, we grow in our love for God and for one another.

QUESTIONS

1. What are some of the false teachings about Jesus you recognize in our world today?

2. Why do you think false teachings so frequently arise in the church?

3. Some people might wonder why it is so important to understand that Jesus was both fully human and fully divine. How would you answer that question?

4. How can we be sure our beliefs about Jesus are correct?

5. What gives you confidence to know you truly belong to God? What can you do if you lack that confidence?

LESSON TWELVE

Living By the Logic of Love and Faith

FOCAL TEXT
1 John 5

BACKGROUND
1 John 5

MAIN IDEA
The intertwining of love for and obedience to God, love for one another, and faith in Jesus as God's Son guides us to victorious Christian living.

QUESTION TO EXPLORE
How can we face life's challenges victoriously and confidently, for now and forever?

STUDY AIM
To affirm or reaffirm my participation in the rich and multifaceted nature of the Christian life

QUICK READ
John shows us practical ways to live in God's love so that our faith in Jesus Christ gives us victory over the world.

I grew up singing "Faith Is the Victory."[1] We sang it in stadiums at evangelistic crusades with thousands of voices and in small one-room churches where men and women rattled the windows with their off-key enthusiasm. "Faith is the victory, that overcomes the world." That is John's message in this passage.[2]

1 JOHN 5

[1] Everyone who believes that Jesus is the Christ is born of God, and everyone who loves the father loves his child as well. [2] This is how we know that we love the children of God: by loving God and carrying out his commands. [3] This is love for God: to obey his commands. And his commands are not burdensome, [4] for everyone born of God overcomes the world. This is the victory that has overcome the world, even our faith. [5] Who is it that overcomes the world? Only he who believes that Jesus is the Son of God. [6] This is the one who came by water and blood—Jesus Christ. He did not come by water only, but by water and blood. And it is the Spirit who testifies, because the Spirit is the truth. [7] For there are three that testify: [8] the Spirit, the water and the blood; and the three are in agreement. [9] We accept man's testimony, but God's testimony is greater because it is the testimony of God, which he has given about his Son. [10] Anyone who believes in the Son of God has this testimony in his heart. Anyone who does not believe God has made him out to be a liar, because he has not believed the testimony God has given about his Son. [11] And this is the testimony: God has given us eternal life, and this life is in his Son. [12] He who has the Son has life; he who does not have the Son of God does not have life. [13] I write these things to you who believe in the name of the Son of God so that you may know that you have eternal life. [14] This is the confidence we have in approaching God: that if we ask anything according to his will, he hears us. [15] And if we know that he hears us—whatever we ask—we know that we have what we asked of him. [16] If anyone sees his brother commit a sin that does not lead to death, he should pray and God will give him life. I refer to those whose sin does not lead to death. There is a sin that leads to death. I am not saying that he should

pray about that. [17] All wrongdoing is sin, and there is sin that does not lead to death. [18] We know that anyone born of God does not continue to sin; the one who was born of God keeps him safe, and the evil one cannot harm him. [19] We know that we are children of God, and that the whole world is under the control of the evil one. [20] We know also that the Son of God has come and has given us understanding, so that we may know him who is true. And we are in him who is true—even in his Son Jesus Christ. He is the true God and eternal life. [21] Dear children, keep yourselves from idols.

Love Is Something You Do (5:1–3)

We are all God's creation. But we are not all God's children. We become children of God by trusting in his Son, Jesus Christ. This makes us part of his family and plants in our hearts a love for God and a love for others. But how do we know we are truly living a life of love toward God?

To answer this question, John echoed words he had heard from the lips of Jesus. From the time John began following Jesus through the Galilean countryside, John heard Jesus link love with obedience to his commands.

Prior to choosing the Twelve, Jesus delivered his Sermon on the Mount (Matthew 5—7), in which he revolutionized all understanding about God and his commandments. Jesus concluded his message with a powerful illustration. He described two men who built houses, one on sand and the other on rock. When the storm came, the house built on sand collapsed. The house built on rock survived. He then made this powerful application: "Therefore everyone who hears these words of mine and puts them into practice is like a wise man who built his house on the rock" (Matt. 7:24). According to Jesus' application, both men had heard his instruction. Both men knew his commands. The difference was that one of them obeyed and put Jesus' instruction into practice.

In the Gospel that bears his name, John recalled Jesus' continued instruction regarding this truth. Once when speaking to a group who said they believed in him, Jesus said, "If you hold to my teaching, you are really my disciples. Then you will know the truth, and the truth will set you free" (John 8:31–32).

What did John have in mind when he urged us to "carry out his commands" (1 John 5:2). Many of us think of religious things. We think of
attending church, giving our tithes and offerings, reading our Bibles,
and observing religious rituals. All of these things are good. But Jesus
didn't say much about them. He attended the synagogues and visited
the temple, even though his home synagogue tried to stone him and
the temple rulers plotted his death. He never, though, measured faith by
attendance at the synagogue or temple.

Surely John had in mind the commands he heard from Jesus. Jesus
chose to focus his commandments on the way we live when we are not
in church. He commanded us to curtail our anger and respect all people;
to be more concerned about our relationship to our brothers and sisters than our religious observances; to avoid lust; to honor and protect
our marriage vows; to tell the truth, a simple *yes* or *no* being sufficient;
to refuse to resist an evil person; to give to those who ask; to love our
enemy; to avoid religious show in our giving, praying, and fasting; to
forgive others their offenses; to avoid letting our possessions control our
lives; to stop worrying and trust God for life's essentials; to refrain from
judgmental attitudes; and to trust in God's goodness (Matt. 5:21—7:9).

The one command of Jesus most Baptists are familiar with is, "Go
therefore and make disciples of all the nations, baptizing them in the
name of the Father and the Son and the Holy Spirit, teaching them to
observe all that I commanded you" (Matthew 28:19–20a, NASB). But
what did Jesus mean when he said this? He was clearly not interested in
sending out his followers to make people more religious. He condemned
the scribes and Pharisees for doing this very thing (Matt. 23:15). He was
also not interested in getting people to merely believe he was the Son of
God. Even the devil and his demons believed (Mark 1:24; James 2:19).

What Jesus meant is very close to what he said. He wanted his followers to become disciples who observed all he commanded them to do. We
have not fulfilled his Great Commission until we are following Jesus'
commands and teaching others to do the same.

Faith Is More Than Feeling (5:4–10)

Faith alone doesn't save anyone. If I place my trust in the wrong object,
I am doomed. One person may put his faith in a well-maintained and

piloted aircraft and fly from one destination to another. Another may put his faith in a plane with mechanical problems and a negligent flight crew. The first successfully arrives at his appointed destination. The second dies in a fiery crash at take-off. Both had faith. But one placed his faith in the wrong object.

John is clear that the only object for our faith that will deliver is Jesus Christ. He can be trusted absolutely. This requires more than giving mental assent that Jesus is the Son of God; this involves trusting our lives to him so we are "born of God" (1 John 5:4). We become changed people who live differently. When the world tells us one thing and Jesus tells us another, we trust Jesus.

John's reference to the water, the blood, and the Spirit echoes the conversation Jesus had with Nicodemus, a respected ruler of the Jews. Recognizing that Nicodemus was a good man and very religious, Jesus told him, "Unless one is born of water and the Spirit he cannot enter into the kingdom of God" (John 3:5, NASB). Jesus continued, "You must be born again" (John 3:7, NASB). The new birth experience comes from God and is made possible by God.

There are several interpretations of what 1 John 5:6–8 might mean. Some seek to interpret it in terms of sacraments administered by the church. It seems to me that John was using water and blood to refer to our natural birth. We all enter this world through the breaking of our mother's water from the womb. We have nothing to do with it. God formed us in the womb, and our mother gave us birth. Everyone who has attended a baby's birth knows it is an event involving both water and blood.

BELIEVE

We often use the term *believe* to indicate mental agreement, such as, *I believe you*. Or, we use it to indicate an opinion that still has some doubt, such as, *I believe that's right, but I'm not sure*. This is not the kind of belief John was describing.

The word John used might better be understood as *trust* or *confidence*. It is the Greek word *pisteuo*. I can believe an airplane will fly, but I don't trust the airplane until I get on board, take my seat, and take off. The kind of believing John describes *gets on board* with Jesus and trusts him completely for everything.

VICTORY

The Greek word for the *victory* that overcomes the world is the word *nike*. The athletic shoe, Nike®, takes its name from this word for *victory* or *conqueror*. Paul used the word *hyper-nike, hupernikomnen*, when he said we are "more than conquerors" in Christ (Romans 8:37).

Likewise, we must all be born again by the Spirit. Jesus emphasized this to Nicodemus. "That which is born of the flesh is flesh, and that which is born of the Spirit is spirit" (John 3:6). When we are born into the world of flesh, we live by the instincts and passions of the flesh. We live like the rest of the world. But when we put our trust in Jesus, God enables us to be born again by the Spirit so that we live by the passions of God and seek the things of God as reflected in Jesus' teaching. When this happens, faith gives us the victory that overcomes the world.

Forever Starts Right Now (5:11–13)

John wanted every born-again believer to know with certainty that he or she has eternal life. John's statement in verse 13 echoes the statement Job discovered in his suffering. Job said, "Oh that my words were written! Oh that they were inscribed in a book! . . . As for me, I know that my Redeemer lives, And at the last He will take His stand on the earth. Even after my skin is destroyed, Yet from my flesh I shall see God; Whom I myself shall behold, And whom my eyes will see and not another" (Job 19:23, 25–27, NASB)

When we know we have eternal life we can endure hardship, personal loss, and catastrophe without losing heart. This confidence gave boldness and courage to the early disciples.

Our confidence in eternal life is not based on emotions or wishful thinking. It is based on the historical resurrection of Jesus from the dead and the promise of God in his word.

We don't have to wait until our physical body dies to start living eternal life. If we have trusted Jesus, our eternal life has already started. Eternal life is a different quality of life than the world knows. It flows out of a personal relationship of trust and faith with Jesus Christ. That is why John said, "He who has the Son has life; he who does not have the Son of God does not life" (1 John 5:12). That is why Jesus said, "Everyone who lives and believes in Me will never die" (John 11:26, NASB).

Life Can Be Lived with Confidence (5:14–21)

All of this gives us confidence for living the transformed life. We have been born again as sons and daughters of God whose passion is to know him, see his glory, and experience his will on earth as it is in heaven. This quality of life goes beyond religion, church attendance, or church membership. It extends into the ages forever.

This quality of life in Jesus Christ changes our prayer life. We no longer pray merely for the things we want or for our own personal interest. We pray according to what Jesus desires. Almost everyone prays. Most pray for their health, for protection from injury or loss, and for their family members and loved ones. It is okay to pray for these things. But until our prayer life goes beyond these interests, we are little different from anyone else. When our prayers take on the character of Jesus' prayer in the garden when he prayed, "Not what I will, but what you will" (Mark 14:36), we enter a new experience.

John's reference to the "sin that does not lead to death" is difficult to understand. He left it without definition, and we are left to conjecture what it might be. The only sin Jesus said would not be forgiven was blasphemy of the Holy Spirit (Mark 3:29; Luke 12:10). It seems to me that blaspheming the Holy Spirit is best understood as rejection of God and his work in Jesus Christ since the Holy Spirit bears witness to Jesus.

APPLICATIONS

- Keep a record of your prayer requests for a week, and examine what you pray for.
- Read the Sermon on the Mount in Matthew 5—7, and list the commands from Jesus that you find.
- List any sins in your life. Confess and repent of these sins, and destroy the list.

The result of being born again as children of God into a trust relationship with Jesus means we are no longer able to continue to live in sin. This does not mean we never sin. We know we do. But it means we cannot continue in that sin since the Holy Spirit convicts of sin and leads us to repentance.

Implications and Actions

If we want to live victorious lives of faith in Jesus Christ, we must follow his instructions and obey his commands. There is no short cut. When we refuse to do what Jesus tells us to do, we are refusing to believe or trust in him. Sometimes his commands are contrary to the world's values. When we refuse to get even with those who wrong us but, instead, forgive them and do good for them, we are following Jesus' commands. When we go against the world's standards and practice what Jesus told us to do, we experience victory and eternal life right here on earth. This kind of life will never die.

QUESTIONS

1. Whom do you know who best exemplifies victorious Christian faith? Why do you think so?

2. Has there ever been a time in your life when you put your trust and faith in Jesus Christ?

3. When you pray, what do you pray for?

4. How do you feel about dying? Do you know you have eternal life? How do you know?

5. If someone were to look for evidence you believe in Jesus, what evidence would they find?

6. Does it matter what you believe just as long as you believe it? Why or why not?

NOTES

1. Words, John H. Yates; music, Ira D. Sankey (1891).

2. Unless otherwise indicated, all Scripture quotations in lessons 12–13 are from the New International Version.

LESSON THIRTEEN
Support God's Work Generously and Wisely

FOCAL TEXT
2 John 1–2, 7–11; 3 John 1–11

BACKGROUND
2 and 3 John

MAIN IDEA
Christians are to support generously and wisely the work of sharing the gospel.

QUESTION TO EXPLORE
How generous and wise are you in supporting the work of sharing the gospel?

STUDY AIM
To decide on ways in which I will increase my support of sharing the gospel

QUICK READ
John's letters affirm a love for the church and support for Christian workers that springs from our love for Christ.

Participation in churches is changing. While the local church has been the *go-to place* for religious experience, today many people are finding alternative expressions for their faith outside the local church. This change means that participating in many things related to the church, including supporting the work of missions, is changing.

We need to ask ourselves some questions like these: *Do we value the church as we need to? How well are we doing at being the church God wants us to be? Are we supporting the work of sharing the gospel?* Second and Third John help us with these questions.

2 JOHN 1–2, 7–11

[1] The elder, To the chosen lady and her children, whom I love in the truth—and not I only, but also all who know the truth— [2] because of the truth, which lives in us and will be with us forever:

. . . .

[7] Many deceivers, who do not acknowledge Jesus Christ as coming in the flesh, have gone out into the world. Any such person is the deceiver and the antichrist. [8] Watch out that you do not lose what you have worked for, but that you may be rewarded fully. [9] Anyone who runs ahead and does not continue in the teaching of Christ does not have God; whoever continues in the teaching has both the Father and the Son. [10] If anyone comes to you and does not bring this teaching, do not take him into your house or welcome him. [11] Anyone who welcomes him shares in his wicked work.

3 JOHN 1–11

[1] The elder, To my dear friend Gaius, whom I love in the truth. [2] Dear friend, I pray that you may enjoy good health and that all may go well with you, even as your soul is getting along well. [3] It gave me great joy to have some brothers come and tell about your faithfulness to the truth and how you continue to walk in the truth. [4] I have no greater joy than to hear that my children are walking in the truth. [5] Dear friend, you are faithful in what you are doing

for the brothers, even though they are strangers to you. [6] They have told the church about your love. You will do well to send them on their way in a manner worthy of God. [7] It was for the sake of the Name that they went out, receiving no help from the pagans. [8] We ought therefore to show hospitality to such men so that we may work together for the truth. [9] I wrote to the church, but Diotrephes, who loves to be first, will have nothing to do with us. [10] So if I come, I will call attention to what he is doing, gossiping maliciously about us. Not satisfied with that, he refuses to welcome the brothers. He also stops those who want to do so and puts them out of the church. [11] Dear friend, do not imitate what is evil but what is good. Anyone who does what is good is from God. Anyone who does what is evil has not seen God.

If We Love Christ, We Will Love the Church (2 John 1–2)

Review the letters in the New Testament, and you will see that in most cases, the opening statement identifies the writer of the letter. One reason for doing this was because their letters were written on scrolls instead of books. A reader could not flip over to the end of the text to see who was writing.

In both 2 John 1 and 3 John 1, the writer is identified as "the elder." My view is that "the elder" is John's reference to himself. The term he used was *presbuteros,* which is most often translated in the New Testament as "elder."

John was an apostle, one of the original twelve disciples of Jesus, one of the inner circle of three along with Peter and James who joined Jesus on the Mount of Transfiguration. He was the author of the Book of Revelation and the Gospel that bears his name. By his own account he was an eyewitness of Jesus' life. He might have chosen to refer to himself as "elder" because of his age.[1] Although John was the youngest of the twelve disciples, he outlived the others and died near the end of the first century.

John addressed 2 John to "the chosen lady." Who was this? John likely used this expression to represent the church.[2] John's devotion and love for the church is also expressed in the Book of Revelation, which he addressed to the seven churches of Asia Minor (Revelation 1:4).

When John spoke of the "chosen lady," he referred to the church as people rather than as an institution. At the end of the first century, the church had no buildings and little organization. Both the polytheistic Romans and the Jewish leaders sought to stamp out the Christian movement. Consequently, Christians met in homes, usually in small groups. As people experienced the transforming power of Jesus Christ, their winsome witness won others, and the church multiplied throughout the Roman Empire. This expression of the "church," which Jesus promised would prevail against the gates of hell (Matthew 16:15–18), transformed the Roman world in which it existed.

The first-century church John knew and to whom he ministered was not perfect. They did not always do what John wanted them to do. There were problems in it that were not unlike problems that crop up in churches today. But John would not give up on loving the church because he was committed to "the truth" (2 John 1–2). John loved the church because of "the truth" he had come to know in Jesus.

Some may ask as Pilate asked Jesus, "What is truth?" (John 18:38). John had no doubt about the answer. He remembered clearly what he heard Jesus say: "I am the way and the truth and the life. No one comes to the

THE BAGBYS OF BRAZIL

In 1880, a young Baptist pastor at Corsicana, Texas, fell in love with the daughter of the president of Baylor University at Independence.[3] William Buck Bagby and Anne Luther were convinced God had called them to carry the gospel to Brazil. They faced a huge problem. They had no money. The Texas Baptist Woman's Missionary Union formed 345 Anne Luther societies in Texas and began to raise the money to send them.[4] The Bagbys married, and soon William resigned his church so he and Anne could seek appointment as missionaries.

The Foreign Mission Board wanted to send them to China. The Bagbys responded that they intended to go to Brazil. They soon sailed for Brazil.[5] In 2007, Brazilian Baptists honored the Bagbys at their 100th anniversary as the founders of their work, reporting 6,500 churches and more than one million members.[6]

Father except through me" (John 14:6), and "You will know the truth and the truth will set you free" (John 8:32). John understood that truth was synonymous with Jesus. John not only heard, saw, and touched "the truth" when he was with Jesus (1 John 1:1–3), but he also experienced "the truth" by faith in Jesus Christ.

If We Love Christ We Will Abide in His Teachings (2 John 7–11)

There have always been Elmer Gantrys, charlatans, and shysters who prey on people's religious emotions to pad their pockets. John encountered his first such deceiver shortly after the resurrection when he and Peter visited Samaria. A popular magician named Simon wanted to *buy* the Holy Spirit. Peter informed him, in no uncertain terms, that the Holy Spirit was not for sale (Acts 8:9–23). Today, whenever those who claim to be spokesmen for God live in luxury with multiple mansions and private jets, something is wrong.

John offered two tests to identify religious deceivers. The first is acknowledging that Jesus Christ came "in the flesh" (2 John 7). Even in John's lifetime, some wanted to make Jesus too spiritual to be human. But John knew otherwise. He lived with Jesus for three years. He saw him, heard him, and touched him (1 John 1:1–3). Jesus, John knew, was a human being. As John put it elsewhere, "And the Word became flesh, and dwelt among us, and we saw His glory, glory as the only begotten from the Father, full of grace and truth" (John 1:14, NASB). Religion tends to make God so otherworldly that we cannot relate to him. Jesus, who was fully human as well as fully divine, forms a unique connection to God for all people. We can relate to him. He can relate to us.

The second test for identifying religious deceivers was whether a person was abiding in the teaching of Jesus. This test takes religion out of the abstract and places it squarely in the concrete. The word translated "abide" (2 John 9, NASB, NRSV) or "continue" (NIV) also means to *live*, to *dwell*, or to *keep*. Anyone who does not practice the teachings of Jesus does not abide in him. Jesus explained this principle clearly in John 15. He used the illustration of a branch that is attached to a tree. If it is lopped off, it withers and dies. In the same way, anyone who does not practice Jesus' teachings is like that branch. Whenever the Christian life, or the church, becomes dull and dry, it can be traced back to this axiom. If we want to experience the life and power of Christ in us, we must abide in him. If we want to abide in him, we must do what he told us to do. Jesus said, "If you keep My commandments you will abide in My love; just as I have kept my Father's commandments and abide in His love" (John 15:10, NASB). If you have any question about what Jesus was referring to as his "commandments," revisit the Sermon on the Mount (Matthew 5—7).

If We Love Christ, We Will Invest in His Church (3 John 1–11)

John addressed 3 John to a believer named Gaius. John, who was now in his old age, considered Gaius to be one of his "children" (3 John 4) in the faith. His reference to the joy he felt when younger believers walk in the truth reminds us of the importance of investing in the next generation.

John encouraged the believers who were with Gaius to generously support other Christian workers. He had heard of their love for a group of Christian workers who had gone out "for the sake of the Name" (3 John 7). He encouraged Gaius to be generous in supporting them. This practice continued the pattern Paul established, working to support himself when necessary but greatly helped by fellow believers who supported his ministry (Romans 15:24; Philippians 4:15–16). Individuals and churches need to practice generous giving in support of the mission of those who serve Christ.

John closed by addressing an internal issue that threatened to disrupt the fellowship and derail the work of the church receiving his letter. Diotrephes was making a power play in the church. In his desire "to be first" (3 John 9), Diotrephes was spreading slanderous rumors about John and his companions in an effort to discredit their ministry (3 John 10). John confronted this behavior and affirmed Demetrius as the person among them who could give good leadership. We may be surprised to discover that churches in the New Testament faced these problems. It is a reminder that most churches, at one time or another, will face such issues. Many Christians prefer to ignore such problems and hope they will go away. But 3 John reminds us that leadership conflicts must be addressed openly and bravely so that the church remains effective in its calling.

APPLYING THE LESSON

- Examine your personal or family budget and determine what percentage is given to support the work of the gospel.
- Look for ways you could increase this percentage in the coming year.
- Find out how much of your church's budget is allocated for churches' working together in missions through the Cooperative Program.
- Look for ways the mission commitment of your church could be increased.

Implications and Actions

The New Testament clearly indicates that churches in the first century had internal problems. These ranged from theological disagreements to leadership conflicts to immorality. Nevertheless John and the other apostles loved the church. In spite of the church's imperfections, God has used the church throughout the centuries to advance the gospel and change the world for the better.

We must never give up on loving the church, helping the church overcome its internal issues, and encouraging the church to generously support the mission of sharing the gospel. We love the church best when we keep our focus on Jesus, walk in the truth, and abide in his teachings.

QUESTIONS

1. What do you love most about your church?

2. How has your church made a difference in your life and that of your family and friends?

3. How is your church engaged in missions in the community and the world, including in cooperative work with other Baptist churches?

4. How can you and your church increase your support for missions?

5. What can you do to create greater harmony in your church?

NOTES ─────────────────────────────────────

1. See also 1 Peter 5:1.

2. Other New Testament references imply the description of the church as *the bride of Christ.* See 2 Corinthians 11:2; Ephesians 5:25; Revelation 19:7–9; 21:2, 9; 22:17.

3. See www.tshaonline.org/handbook/online/articles/BB/fbada.html. Accessed 4/23/10. See also Justice C. Anderson, *An Evangelical Saga: Baptists and Their Precursors in Latin America* (Longwood, Florida: Xulon Press, 2005), 136–138. Search for *An Evangelical Saga* at www.google.com/books. Accessed 4/23/10.

4. See www.tshaonline.org/handbook/online/articles/TT/ixtcy.html. Accessed 4/23/10.

5. Daniel B. Lancaster, *The Bagbys of Brazil* (Waco, Texas: Eakin Press, 1999), 24.

6. See www.christiantoday.com/article/brazilian.baptist.convention.celebrates.centennial.anniversary/9486.htm. Accessed 4/23/10.

Our Next New Study

(Available for use beginning December 2010)

THE GOSPEL OF JOHN:
Light Overcoming Darkness
Part One—The Light Shines (John 1—12)

Additional Resources for Studying the Gospel of John

George R. Beasley-Murray. *John*. Word Biblical Commentary. Volume 36. Waco, Texas: Word Books, Publisher, 1987.

Raymond E. Brown. *The Gospel According to John (I—XII)*. Garden City, New York: Doubleday & Company, Inc., 1966.

Raymond E. Brown. *The Gospel According to John (XIII—XXI)*. Garden City, New York: Doubleday & Company, Inc., 1970.

F.F. Bruce. *The Gospel of John*. Grand Rapids, Michigan: William B. Eerdmans Publishing Company, 1983.

Gary M. Burge, *The NIV Application Commentary: John*. Grand Rapids, Michigan: Zondervan Publishing House, 2000.

James E. Carter. *John*. Layman's Bible Book Commentary. Volume 18. Nashville: Broadman Press, 1984.

Herschel H. Hobbs. *The Gospel of John: Invitation to Life*. Nashville, Tennessee: Convention Press, 1988.

William E. Hull. "John." *The Broadman Bible Commentary*. Volume 9. Nashville, Tennessee: Broadman Press, 1970.

Craig S. Keener. *The Gospel of John: A Commentary*. Two volumes. Peabody, Massachusetts: Hendrickson Publishers, 2003.

Lesslie Newbigin. *The Light Has Come: An Exposition of the Fourth Gospel*. Grand Rapids, Michigan: William B. Eerdmans Publishing Company, 1982.

Gail R. O'Day. "The Gospel of John." *The New Interpreter's Bible*. Volume IX. Nashville, Tennessee: Abingdon Press, 1995.

Additional Future Adult Bible Studies

The Gospel of John: Part Two (John 13—21)	For use beginning March 2011
Models of Character	For use beginning May 22, 2011

How to Order More Bible Study Materials

It's easy! Just fill in the following information. For additional Bible study materials available both in print and online, see www.baptistwaypress.org, or get a complete order form of available print materials—including Spanish materials—by calling 1-866-249-1799 or e-mailing baptistway@bgct.org.

Title of item	Price	Quantity	Cost
This Issue:			
Letters of James and John—Study Guide (BWP001101)	$3.55		
Letters of James and John—Large Print Study Guide (BWP001102)	$3.95		
Letters of James and John—Teaching Guide (BWP001103)	$4.25		
Additional Issues Available:			
Growing Together in Christ—Study Guide (BWP001036)	$3.25		
Growing Together in Christ—Teaching Guide (BWP001038)	$3.75		
Living Faith in Daily Life—Study Guide (BWP001095)	$3.55		
Living Faith in Daily Life—Large Print Study Guide (BWP001096)	$3.95		
Living Faith in Daily Life—Teaching Guide (BWP001097)	$4.25		
Participating in God's Mission—Study Guide (BWP001077)	$3.55		
Participating in God's Mission—Large Print Study Guide (BWP001078)	$3.95		
Participating in God's Mission—Teaching Guide (BWP001079)	$3.95		
Genesis: People Relating to God—Study Guide (BWP001088)	$2.35		
Genesis: People Relating to God—Large Print Study Guide (BWP001089)	$2.75		
Genesis: People Relating to God—Teaching Guide (BWP001090)	$2.95		
Genesis 12—50: Family Matters—Study Guide (BWP000034)	$1.95		
Genesis 12—50: Family Matters—Teaching Guide (BWP000035)	$2.45		
Leviticus, Numbers, Deuteronomy—Study Guide (BWP000053)	$2.35		
Leviticus, Numbers, Deuteronomy—Large Print Study Guide (BWP000052)	$2.35		
Leviticus, Numbers, Deuteronomy—Teaching Guide (BWP000054)	$2.95		
1 and 2 Samuel—Study Guide (BWP000002)	$2.35		
1 and 2 Samuel—Large Print Study Guide (BWP000001)	$2.35		
1 and 2 Samuel—Teaching Guide (BWP000003)	$2.95		
1 and 2 Kings: Leaders and Followers—Study Guide (BWP001025)	$2.95		
1 and 2 Kings: Leaders and Followers Large Print Study Guide (BWP001026)	$3.15		
1 and 2 Kings: Leaders and Followers Teaching Guide (BWP001027)	$3.45		
Ezra, Haggai, Zechariah, Nehemiah, Malachi—Study Guide (BWP001071)	$3.25		
Ezra, Haggai, Zechariah, Nehemiah, Malachi—Large Print Study Guide (BWP001072)	$3.55		
Ezra, Haggai, Zechariah, Nehemiah, Malachi—Teaching Guide (BWP001073)	$3.75		
Job, Ecclesiastes, Habakkuk, Lamentations—Study Guide (BWP001016)	$2.75		
Job, Ecclesiastes, Habakkuk, Lamentations—Large Print Study Guide (BWP001017)	$2.85		
Job, Ecclesiastes, Habakkuk, Lamentations—Teaching Guide (BWP001018)	$3.25		
Psalms and Proverbs—Study Guide (BWP001000)	$2.75		
Psalms and Proverbs—Teaching Guide (BWP001002)	$3.25		
Matthew: Hope in the Resurrected Christ—Study Guide (BWP001066)	$3.25		
Matthew: Hope in the Resurrected Christ—Large Print Study Guide (BWP001067)	$3.55		
Matthew: Hope in the Resurrected Christ—Teaching Guide (BWP001068)	$3.75		
Mark: Jesus' Works and Words—Study Guide (BWP001022)	$2.95		
Mark: Jesus' Works and Words—Large Print Study Guide (BWP001023)	$3.15		
Mark:Jesus' Works and Words—Teaching Guide (BWP001024)	$3.45		
Jesus in the Gospel of Mark—Study Guide (BWP000066)	$1.95		
Jesus in the Gospel of Mark—Teaching Guide (BWP000067)	$2.45		
Luke: Journeying to the Cross—Study Guide (BWP000057)	$2.35		
Luke: Journeying to the Cross—Large Print Study Guide (BWP000056)	$2.35		
Luke: Journeying to the Cross—Teaching Guide (BWP000058)	$2.95		
The Gospel of John: The Word Became Flesh—Study Guide (BWP001008)	$2.75		
The Gospel of John: The Word Became Flesh—Large Print Study Guide (BWP001009)	$2.85		
The Gospel of John: The Word Became Flesh—Teaching Guide (BWP001010)	$3.25		
Acts: Toward Being a Missional Church—Study Guide (BWP001013)	$2.75		
Acts: Toward Being a Missional Church—Large Print Study Guide (BWP001014)	$2.85		
Acts: Toward Being a Missional Church—Teaching Guide (BWP001015)	$3.25		
Romans: What God Is Up To—Study Guide (BWP001019)	$2.95		
Romans: What God Is Up To—Large Print Study Guide (BWP001020)	$3.15		
Romans: What God Is Up To—Teaching Guide (BWP001021)	$3.45		
Galatians and 1&2 Thessalonians—Study Guide (BWP001080)	$3.55		
Galatians and 1&2 Thessalonians—Large Print Study Guide (BWP001081)	$3.95		
Galatians and 1&2 Thessalonians—Teaching Guide (BWP001082)	$3.95		

Ephesians, Philippians, Colossians—Study Guide (BWP001060) $3.25   _____   _____
Ephesians, Philippians, Colossians—Large Print Study Guide (BWP001061) $3.55   _____   _____
Ephesians, Philippians, Colossians—Teaching Guide (BWP001062) $3.75   _____   _____
1, 2 Timothy, Titus, Philemon—Study Guide (BWP000092) $2.75   _____   _____
1, 2 Timothy, Titus, Philemon—Large Print Study Guide (BWP000091) $2.85   _____   _____
1, 2 Timothy, Titus, Philemon—Teaching Guide (BWP000093) $3.25   _____   _____
Revelation—Study Guide (BWP000084) $2.35   _____   _____
Revelation—Large Print Study Guide (BWP000083) $2.35   _____   _____
Revelation—Teaching Guide (BWP000085) $2.95   _____   _____

Coming for use beginning December 2010

The Gospel of John: Light Overcoming Darkness,
Part One—Study Guide (BWP001104) $3.55   _____   _____

The Gospel of John: Light Overcoming Darkness,
Part One—Large Print Study Guide (BWP001105) $3.95   _____   _____

The Gospel of John: Light Overcoming Darkness,
Part One—Teaching Guide (BWP001106) $4.50   _____   _____

Standard (UPS/Mail) Shipping Charges*			
Order Value	Shipping charge**	Order Value	Shipping charge**
$.01—$9.99	$6.50	$160.00—$199.99	$22.00
$10.00—$19.99	$8.00	$200.00—$249.99	$26.00
$20.00—$39.99	$9.00	$250.00—$299.99	$28.00
$40.00—$59.99	$10.00	$300.00—$349.99	$32.00
$60.00—$79.99	$11.00	$350.00—$399.99	$40.00
$80.00—$99.99	$12.00	$400.00—$499.99	$48.00
$100.00—$129.99	$14.00	$500.00—$599.99	$58.00
$130.00—$159.99	$18.00	$600.00—$799.99	$70.00**

Cost
of items (Order value)   _____

Shipping charges
(see chart*)   _____

TOTAL   _____

*Plus, applicable taxes for individuals and other taxable entities (not churches) within Texas will be added. Please call 1-866-249-1799 if the exact amount is needed prior to ordering.

**For order values $800.00 and above, please call 1-866-249-1799 or check www.baptistwaypress.org

Please allow three weeks for standard delivery. For express shipping service: Call 1-866-249-1799 for information on additional charges.

YOUR NAME   PHONE

YOUR CHURCH   DATE ORDERED

SHIPPING ADDRESS

CITY   STATE   ZIP CODE

E-MAIL

MAIL this form with your check for the total amount to
BAPTISTWAY PRESS, Baptist General Convention of Texas,
333 North Washington, Dallas, TX 75246-1798
(Make checks to "Baptist Executive Board.")

OR, **FAX** your order anytime to: 214-828-5376, and we will bill you.

OR, **CALL** your order toll-free: 1-866-249-1799
(M-Th 8:30 a.m.-6:00 p.m.; Fri 8:30 a.m.-5:00 p.m. central time),
and we will bill you.

OR, **E-MAIL** your order to our internet e-mail address:
baptistway@texasbaptists.org, and we will bill you.

OR, **ORDER ONLINE** at www.baptistwaypress.org.

We look forward to receiving your order! Thank you!